THE COMMON PEOPLE'S GOSPEL

THE COMMON PEOPLE'S GOSPEL

by

Gunpei Yamamuro

Salvation Books
The Salvation Army International Headquarters
London, United Kingdom

First published 1899

Revised edition 1988
This edition 2008
Copyright © 2008
The General of The Salvation Army

ISBN 978-0-85412-771-9

Cover design by Nathan Sigauke

Published by Salvation Books
The Salvation Army International Headquarters
101 Queen Victoria Street, London EC4V 4EH
United Kingdom

Printed by UK Territory Print & Design Unit

CONTENTS

Page

Author's Preface	vii
Expression of Thanks	viii
Editor's Note	ix
Revising Editor's Note	x

CHAPTER 1:
OUR FATHER IN HEAVEN ... 1
   Faith in God is natural to human beings ... 1
   When you cross a stone bridge, be sure it is safe! ... 4
   In the beginning God created the heavens and the earth ... 7
   God is the Father of all mankind ... 11
   God must be worshipped in spirit and in truth ... 13

CHAPTER 2:
THE SIN OF MANKIND ... 19
   There is none righteous; no, not one ... 19
   Sin is the source of all misfortune ... 23
   Sin affects the body ... 23
   Sin affects the heart ... 24
   Sin determines the soul's destiny ... 25
   Sin multiplies ... 26
   Man cannot save himself ... 30
   Repent and return to a Heavenly Father ... 34

Page

CHAPTER 3:
SALVATION THROUGH CHRIST   39
  Jesus Christ is the Son of God   39
  Christ is the Saviour of all mankind   43
  Behold, now is the day of salvation   47
  That which is born of the Spirit is spirit   51
  The religion of Christ is the religion of victory 54
  Burying Satan   56
  Satan buried again   58

CHAPTER 4:
THE CHRISTIAN LIFE   61
  Prayer is important   62
  Read the Bible   67
  Riseko Morita – a pious woman   71
  Show your colours   73
  Fighting the good fight of faith   78
  An exemplary soldier   83
  Receive the Holy Spirit   87

CHAPTER 5:
THE CHRISTIAN'S RESPONSIBILITY   93
  You are the salt of the earth   94
  Seek first the Kingdom of God   98
  Salvation means good health   103
  Love begins at home   106
  To die is gain   113

AUTHOR'S PREFACE

When I was 16 years of age I was a labourer working in a printing factory at Tsukiji, Tokyo, Japan. At that time I experienced salvation through faith in Jesus Christ, and dedicated my life to God. That was 13 years ago. I am now serving God as an officer in The Salvation Army, and the one desire of my heart has been to let you, my beloved people, know of the great love of God.

In one of my songs I have written:

> *Wake up the sleeping souls*
> *With news of God's salvation;*
> *Do not neglect to warn them*
> *Of evil's deprivation.*

Such thoughts compelled me to produce this book, although I do not profess to be a writer.

Gunpei Yamamuro
from a tenement house at Kanda Misakicho
October 1899

EXPRESSION OF THANKS

For some years it has been felt desirable that *The Common People's Gospel* should be translated into English for so many more Salvationists who would love to share the contents of a literary work that has sold 3,000,000 copies in Japan.

We are grateful to Commissioner Robert Rightmire and Commissioner David Ramsay for their help in the preparation of this manuscript during their tenure in Japan.

Sincere appreciation, however, must be expressed to Mrs Major Kazuko Harita for constant application of her mind and energy to the work of translation from the original Japanese, without which this publication would not be possible.

Lastly, my deep gratitude to Retired General Arnold Brown for so willingly agreeing to edit this work, giving to us, at last, an insight into the mind of the revered leader of The Salvation Army in Japan, Commissioner Gunpei Yamamuro, and with such colour and expertise that will enable the English-speaking world also to benefit from this 'Gospel for the Common Man'.

May the blessing of God and spiritual understanding come to all who read this book!

Commissioner Hiroshi Asano
TERRITORIAL COMMANDER
Tokyo, Japan
November 1988

EDITOR'S NOTE

The author, the revered Commissioner Gunpei Yamamuro, was Japanese, and *The Common People's Gospel* was, of course, written in his own language. A translation into English was put into my hands by Colonel David Ramsay (then Territorial Commander for Japan) in the hope that I might find time to shape it into literary English.

I knew that millions of copies of the *Gospel* had been distributed, and there was a natural curiosity on my part to read something that had had such a profound effect for good on so many of Yamamuro's countrymen. The first manuscript made this possible. Because I knew how consequential was the life and work of the author, and because of my abiding affection for my Japanese fellow-Salvationists, I felt honoured to be asked to undertake the task.

The work was more difficult than I anticipated. The Japanese language has its own vast imagery and a generous store of colloquialisms. While I wanted to make the idioms that were used clearly understood, I also wanted the edited version to retain the oriental 'flavour' of the original. Many of the illustrations used by the author belong to other days. Nevertheless, for all their quaintness, they have the sharpness of a samurai's sword in the way in which they slash through sophistication or indifference to expose basic spiritual truths.

Arnold Brown, General (Retired)
1988

REVISING EDITOR'S NOTE

One-time Prime Minister of the United Kingdom Harold Wilson declared: 'A week is a long time in politics.' It is now 20 years since General Arnold Brown produced his edited version of this book – and two decades is a long time when it comes to popular culture and literary style. This new edition has therefore been further revised to replace vocabulary and expressions of thought which have changed in meaning or nuance over those 20 years, and the Bible quotations are now from the *New International Version*. General Brown – one of The Salvation Army's all-time great communicators, now promoted to Glory – would surely have approved.

Charles King, Major
Literary Secretary, International Headquarters
2008

One

Our Father in Heaven

Faith in God is natural to human beings
Higashi Honganji Temple, in Kyoto, has been damaged by fire several times. Someone cynically wrote: 'Honganji Temple was built, destroyed by fire, then rebuilt. This will be repeated as long as there is money.' The last rebuilding of the temple took 17 years, a great deal of effort and a tremendous amount of money. To help, women offered their beautiful long hair to make ropes to pull timbers from the mountains. They wanted to demonstrate the strength of their faith. There are 53 ropes made of women's hair in the Honganji Temple. The thickest is 10.6 metres in length, with a circumference of nearly 40 cm. The thinnest is 34.5 metres long, with a circumference of 13.3 cm. The total weight of the ropes is nearly 4,000 kg. What a lot of hair! Those who offered it were fervent believers.

The believing heart has great power. When the heart is aflame, astonishing things can be accomplished. Just as women offered their hair to Honganji Temple, many men and women have made significant sacrifices for their faith, some yielding their lives. Nothing has greater power than a believing heart, and every human being has a heart with which to believe in God.

On the other hand, many people simply live as they want. Granted good health and wealth and power, they forget about God. They have no faith, and give little thought to the question of sin or the matter of life after death. But great numbers of them, when they fall ill or experience some kind of suffering, come to their senses and start to believe in God.

There are those who once threw stones at church windows but who, after experiencing suffering, began to attend church and pay heed to the pastor's messages. There are those who ridiculed religion saying, 'There is no God,' but who, following a period of tribulation, started to go to the temple or the shrine every day.

A scholar named Balney was travelling by steamship when a fierce storm arose and the vessel almost capsized. Balney was not a religious man and used to say there was no God. But when he found himself in mortal danger he shouted the prayer, 'O God, save me!' The storm abated and the ship returned safely to port. Thereafter the word spread that 'Balney's atheism is wonderful on the shore, but of no use on the sea.'

Those who disdain faith and are very vocal about it are often like lions at home and mice abroad. All is well when they are on the shore, in good weather, with enough money and in good health. But when the wind blows from the opposite direction, they begin to pray to God. It has been said: 'One always has faith in God when in difficulty, and even the atheist has faith in God at midnight.' When people think everything is going well and they are prospering, and there is no cause for worry, disaster can be underfoot. If a man neglects God when he is well, and starts to have faith in God only when he becomes sick, or poor or unhappy, that is a reproach to God and reveals the man's self-centredness. We should repair the roof before the rains come. We should prepare our winter clothes before the cold weather arrives. In the same way we have to make up our minds regarding the most important matter of our lives – the placing of our faith in God. We should do it while we are in good health, and before we reach the lowest rung of misfortune. Life's most important obligation is to find God, and faith in him is surely worthwhile.

'As the deer pants for streams of water, so my soul pants for you, O God. My soul thirsts for God, for the living God. When can I go and meet with God?' (Psalm 42:1, 2). 'Seek the LORD while he may be found; call on him while he is near. Let the wicked forsake his way and the evil man his thoughts. Let him turn to the LORD, and he will have mercy on him, and to our God, for he will freely pardon' (Isaiah 55:6, 7).

When you cross a stone bridge, be sure it is safe!
It is a natural thing for a man to have faith in God. But there are many who, without investigation, will believe anything. They will even worship the head of a small sardine. They worship wooden statues, golden statues, foxes, wolves, anything. If a housewife sends her child to buy tofu (bean curd), she makes sure that the child will get to the shop safely, that the money will not be lost and that the child will bring back the tofu undamaged. One needs faith in a God to whom one is able to trust one's health, soul and eternal life. It is possible for us to make sure who God is, and that he is able to meet our needs.

A European was carried on a palanquin over Mount Hakone. On the way he spoke to the palanquin bearer, but the man could not understand the European's language. The European then wrote some words on a piece of paper and handed it to the bearer who afterwards took it home. He thought it might be some kind of incantation and, being of the Shinto faith, he put it on the family altar. When a scholar who could read English came to the village, the bearer asked him to translate it. On the paper was written, 'Mount Fuji is beautiful.'

The words were nothing special. Is it not so that often the statue which people set up on their family altar and worship is nothing special in itself? Even insects and birds become the gods of the people when they worship them. But why should God's highest creation, man, who has been given dominion over all living things, worship insects and birds? Of the ascetics who are often worshipped someone has said, 'Be careful of the hermits. Most of them are foxes in clothes.'

In one particular shrine people thought the flower arrangement was of special value because, without anyone touching them, the flowers moved. One day, to their surprise, the vase fell over. Out crawled a cockroach!

There is a familiar saying: 'When you cross a stone bridge, be sure it is safe!' Because the putting of our faith in God will be the most important step in our lives, it is necessary for us to be careful. We should make sure we know what kind of God he is, and what our response to him should be. It is a grave mistake to believe in a god simply because that god was handed down from generation to generation, as it was in my own home, or simply because many people also believe in that particular god.

A newly-enrolled Salvation Army soldier gave his testimony in the following words: 'As I was born in Kanda, Tokyo, I belonged to the Kanda Myojin god, and as a boy I went to the shrine whenever there were festivals. Kanda Myojin's god was a military general of olden times, Taira no Masakado. He was killed when rebelling against the authorities, and his body, without a head, it is said, was enshrined. In Asakusa, Tokyo, there is a shrine where the bodies of drowning victims were placed. There is even a tomb in which a notorious thief is enshrined, and to which many come to worship. How foolish to worship like this! I knew that faith is very important, but I could not make up my mind which god to believe in. But now,' concluded the convert, 'I know that the true and living God created the whole universe, and I have faith in him.'

'He cut down cedars, or perhaps took a cypress or oak. He let it grow among among the trees of the forest, or planted a pine, and the rain made it grow. It is man's fuel for burning; some of it he takes and warms himself, he kindles a fire and bakes bread. But he also fashions a god and worships it; he makes an idol and bows down to it. Half of the wood he burns in the fire; over it he prepares his meal, he roasts his meat and eats his fill. He also warms himself and says, "Ah! I am warm; I see the fire." From the rest he makes a god, his idol; he bows down to it and worships. He prays to it and says, "Save me; you are my god." They know nothing, they understand nothing; their eyes are plastered over so that they cannot see, and their minds closed so that they cannot understand. No one stops to think, no one has the knowledge or understanding to say, "Half of it I used for fuel; I even baked bread over its coals, I roasted meat and I ate. Shall I make a detestable thing from what is left? Shall I bow down to a block of wood? He feeds on ashes, a deluded heart misleads him; he cannot save himself, or say, "Is not this thing in my right hand a lie?'" (Isaiah 44:14-20).

In the beginning God created the heavens and the earth

What is this true God, the only one in whom it is worth one's while to believe? What is this God like? He is the God who created all things – mountains, rivers, grass, trees, birds, beasts, human beings and all other things. Trace back your parents, and their parents, and your parents' parents. Where did our first ancestors come from? The true God created our first ancestors and made them to bear children and grandchildren. He provided milk for the infants and food for the adults.

A chick comes out of an egg, and an egg is laid by a grown-up chick – a hen. In the beginning the true God made the hen to lay an egg. We cannot see our soul with the natural eye, neither can we see God. But we know we have a soul because our body moves in response to its direction. Similarly, if we observe everything around us, the heavens and the earth, we know it is God's handiwork.

A thief went into a native American's home and took away the beef that was hanging from a beam in the house. When the native returned he saw that the beef had been stolen. After looking around, the native said: 'The thief must be a short, old, white man with a gun and with a small dog that has a short tail.' He sought out and found the thief and retrieved the beef. His neighbours asked him, 'How could you know who the thief was without seeing him?' He answered: 'A footstool was used to get the beef down from the beam, so I thought the thief must have been a short man. His footprints in the sand were not wide, so I assumed he was an old man. The outside of the footprints were pressed harder into the sand than the inside. That told me he was a white man. A part of the wall had been damaged because someone had stood a gun against it. When I looked at the marks in the dust I knew the man had brought with him a small dog with a short tail.'

Like the native American who, without seeing the thief, could say what kind of man the robber was, we too, though we cannot see God with the natural eye, can understand, when we view the vastness of the universe, that God is almighty. When we consider the unfailing balance maintained between the sun, moon and stars; when we reflect on the complex structure of the human body; we see how great is the wisdom of God. When we think of the sun shining and the rain failing on both the righteous and the unrighteous, we feel that the love of God is all-embracing. When we remember that through conscience we have the means to know right from wrong, we can accept that the true God is a righteous being.

George Washington's father was a sincere Christian and wanted to teach his son that there was a God of creation. He ploughed up part of the garden and sowed seeds in the shape of his son's name. Later there appeared fresh green plants spelling out 'George Washington'. Young George, playing in the garden, suddenly saw his name and rushed to his father. 'Who did it?' he asked. 'Plants don't usually grow in that order. Someone must have planted the seeds in such a way. Did you do it, father?'

The father smiled and answered, 'When you saw your name you immediately thought that someone had planted the seeds to produce the effect. So, when we think of our universe with everything in perfect balance and lacking nothing, how can we not accept that the true and living God created everything in his full wisdom?' Young George was deeply impressed, and with faith in God he lived the life of a fine Christian, following God's will and faithfully doing his duty.

A European scientist has said: 'If there is an astronomer who studies the beautiful moon and stars and does not have faith in God as creator, he is a madman.' The Bible says: 'For since the creation of the world God's invisible qualities – his eternal power and divine nature – have been clearly seen, being understood from what has been made, so that men are without excuse' (Romans 1:20).

Jo Niijima read a book about Christianity when he was 18 or 19 years of age. The book began with the words: 'In the beginning God created the heavens and the earth.' As he read the book he thought, 'It is true that everything in this world has been created by God. A desk is made by a carpenter, but neither the carpenter himself nor the wood he used were made by any human being. As the book says, there must be one true God who has created Heaven and earth, and he must be governing all things.'

Faith in God arose in Niijima's heart. There and then he knelt down and prayed: 'O God, you must be looking at me with your eyes, and with your ears you must be listening to my voice. Please hear my prayer.' Later, Niijima went to America and studied there for many years. When he returned to Japan he bore effective witness to the one true God whom he now served. Let us have faith in the God who created Heaven and earth. He is the only true God worthy of our trust. There is no other god but the Lord of all creation whom we should worship.

'The God who made the world and everything in it is the Lord of Heaven and earth and does not live in temples built by hands. And he is not served by human hands, as if he needed anything, because he himself gives all men life and breath and everything else. From one man he made every nation of men, that they should inhabit the whole earth; and he determined the times set for them and the exact places where they should live. God did this so that men would seek him and perhaps reach out for him and find him, though he is not far from each one of us. "For in him we live and move and have our being." As some of your own poets have said, "We are his offspring"' (Acts 17:24-28).

God is the Father of all mankind

There is one head in a family, one chief in a village, one emperor in a country and one God who rules over Heaven and earth. This true God has all wisdom and power. He is full of mercy and loves us as his children. Alas, we often forget about his grace and blessings and think only of ourselves. This is a dangerous way of life. Even though we are taught about God we sometimes feel far from him.

A friend of mine left his family in the country and came to Tokyo where he spent several years. He then called all his family to join him. The man's son, now eight years of age, was seen looking at his face in the mirror every day, and the father wondered why the boy was so interested in staring at himself. The boy replied, 'I'm not sure whether you are my true father or not. I feel that you are, but I'm not sure. If you are my true father then I will bear some resemblance to you. So I look at my face in the mirror, and then I look at yours.'

The illustration fits. If we have been far from God our Father, and have lived for many years among idols and false gods, it is difficult to identify our true Father and to see any likeness to him. Yet if we take time to think about it we see that we have wisdom, as God has all wisdom; that we have discernment to judge what is right and what is wrong, as God himself is all righteous; and that we have a heart with which to love others, as God himself is full of love. Even if our heart is clouded by sin, we have the image of God in our heart.

Human beings were made in the image of God, and we are his children. Moreover, God has so richly blessed us that we cannot tell how great his grace to us has been. Just as a baby is loved and cared for by its parents, God has blessed and cared for us.

The greatest scholar or scientist finds it impossible to create a cupful of water out of nothing. But God generously gives us the water with which to wash our faces, to have a bath, to drink, to wash our clothes. No matter how hard the farmer worked, he could not produce enough rice or wheat if God did not cause the plants to grow or withheld the good weather and the rain. We might complain that the price of the rice or wheat is too high or too low, but without the grace of God there would be no rice or wheat to complain about. As one grain of rice or wheat shows, we depend utterly on God's grace.

Is it not exceedingly difficult for a person to comprehend fully the love and care his parents gave him when an infant? It is much easier for him to say, 'Thank you!' to someone who gives him a meal now. To someone who strikes a match so a man can see to mend his sandal straps in the dark night it is easy to say, 'Thank you!' Then why should it be so difficult to say 'Thank you!' to the God who by the sun provides light for the whole of the day? How understanding we need to be about such things!

An evangelist was riding on horseback along a country road. From out of a dilapidated house he heard a voice saying, 'O God, you have given me so many wonderful blessings, and now you have given me this precious gift.' The evangelist looked over the fence into the house and saw a man thanking God for the cup of cold water on the table before him.

If we think of it, even a cup of cold water speaks of God's limitless generosity. Just as the earth is surrounded by the air that sustains life, so are we human beings surrounded by the love of God which sustains our spiritual life. 'The Lord is my shepherd, I shall not be in want. He makes me lie down in green pastures, he leads me beside quiet waters, he restores my soul. He guides me in all paths of righteousness for his name's sake. Even though I walk through the valley of the shadow of death, I will fear no evil, for you are with me; your rod and your staff, they comfort me. You prepare a table before me in the presence of my enemies. You anoint my head with oil; my cup overflows. Surely goodness and love will follow me all the days of my life, and I will dwell in the house of the LORD for ever' (Psalm 23).

God must be worshipped in spirit and in truth

Once we know that the God whom we should worship is the creator of Heaven and earth, and is also our Heavenly Father, we must know how to worship him.

People have been known to worship their gods in quite foolish ways. At the shrine of Asakusa Kwannon a man from a country village wept as he prayed: 'O Kwannon, I sent my son to Tokyo for training. The other day he wrote that he was seriously ill and destitute. I sent him money, but in order to do this my wife gave up taking nutritious food. When I went to Tokyo to see our son I found him in good health, but with evil companions. They had led him to spend all his money on prostitutes. He had deceived us. Kwannon, I pray that you will change our son's ways, and his character.'

By the side of this man another man prayed. He had grown rich and fat on the earnings of the prostitutes. In a loud voice he petitioned: 'I pray, Kwannon, that our business might prosper with many more good customers. If you will grant us a 15,000 yen profit this month I will repaper the big lantern at the gate.' Which prayer would Kwannon answer? Would he provide more customers for the prostitutes, or change the prodigal into a righteous man?

It is said that Toyokawa Inari (the god of harvest) will help him who comes first to pray. If a person whose house is burgled comes first to pray to Inari, then the god will catch the robber. But if the burglar is the first to come to Inari and pray, then the robber will never be caught. Such a god, surely, is without reason.

A policeman passing through a temple precinct found a young man praying in front of the tomb of a notorious thief. He was praying so earnestly that the policeman asked him what he was praying for. The man confessed that he could not successfully manage his business. In his despair he had made up his mind to become a thief. He had come to the thief's tomb to pray for help in stealing successfully. One person prays that he might steal without being apprehended. Another prays that he might win the lottery. Another prays for happiness without making any effort to ensure it.

The prostitute, gambler, usurer, rascal, swindler, laggard, thinks it is enough to light a candle, offer some money and pray to any kind of a god, assuming the god will answer his or her prayer. Such worship is senseless and contemptible. Worshipping gods made of wood, or stone, or some other material which can be touched, is false. When we worship the true, spiritual God we must worship him in spirit and in truth. The true God knows everything. He sees everything. He is righteous and holy. If we worship him in truth then we must not tell lies, or steal, or live immorally. We must fear God and try to live according to his will.

A man took his son into a neighbour's field. 'Stand here and watch,' he told the boy, 'while I steal some vegetables. If anyone comes, let me know.' The boy, who faithfully attended Sunday school and knew about the true God, was saddened by his father's words and actions. He stood silently for a time, then shouted: 'Father, someone is looking at you. God in Heaven is looking at us.' The boy then told his father that even when people do not see, God sees and knows everything, and men should not do what they know to be wrong. That boy knew how to worship God.

There is a parable in the Bible about two men who went into the Temple to pray. One was a Pharisee who, like others of his sect, was proud of his religious life. The other was a tax-gatherer. The Pharisee prayed loudly: '"God, I thank you that I am not like other men – robbers, evil-doers, adulterers – or even like this tax collector. I fast twice a week and give a tenth of all I get." But the tax collector stood at a distance. He would not even look up to heaven, but beat his breast and said, "God have mercy on me, a sinner"' (Luke 18:11-14).

The Bible says that God did not accept the arrogant prayer of the Pharisee, but that of the honest, sincere and repentant publican. 'But he gives us more grace. That is why Scripture says: "God opposes the proud but gives grace to the humble."' (James 4:6). 'Man looks at the outward appearance, but the LORD looks at the heart' (1 Samuel 16:7). First, we must humble ourselves. We must repent of our sins and seek divine forgiveness. Having become a new person we must then worship God in spirit and in truth.

'Stop bringing meaningless offerings! Your incense is detestable to me. New Moons, Sabbaths and convocations – I cannot bear your evil assemblies. Your New Moon festivals and your appointed feasts my soul hates. They have become a burden to me; I am weary of bearing them. When you spread out your hands in prayer, I will hide my eyes from you; even if you offer many prayers, I will not listen. Your hands are full of blood; wash and make yourselves clean. Take your evil deeds out of my sight! Stop doing wrong, learn to do right! Seek justice, encourage the oppressed. Defend the cause of the fatherless, plead the case of the widow' (Isaiah 1:13-17).

'Yet a time is coming and has now come when the true worshippers will worship the Father in spirit and truth, for they are the kind of worshippers the Father seeks. God is spirit, and his worshippers must worship in spirit and in truth' (John 4:23, 24).

Two

The sin of mankind

There is none righteous; no, not one
'Why do you look at the speck of sawdust in your brother's eye and pay no attention to the plank in your own eye? How can you say to your brother, "Let me take the speck out of your eye," when all the time there is a plank in your own eye? You hypocrite, first take the plank out of your own eye, and then you will see clearly to remove the speck from your brother's eye' (Matthew 7:3-5).

The Bible reproves the hypocrite. Shallow and superficial unbelievers see only the faults of others, but sincere people can acknowledge their own sins. By sins we do not mean crimes committed against the nation's laws, but rather those thoughts, words and deeds which are against one's conscience and which pain the heart of God.

'All wrongdoing is sin, and there is sin that does not lead to death' (1 John 5:17). 'But the man who has doubts is condemned if he eats, because his eating is not from faith; and everything that does not come from faith is sin' (Romans 14:23). 'Anyone, then, who knows the good he ought to do and doesn't do it, sins' (James 4:17).

Quarrelling, speaking ill of others, holding grudges, being jealous, greedy, proud, untruthful, deceitful, unfaithful, ungrateful, unkind, intemperate, cruel, impious, idle, wasteful; gambling and drunkenness – all are sins before God. Applying these measures to ourselves, no one can say, 'I have never sinned.' 'There is no one righteous, not even one' (Romans 3:10). All are sinners before God.

A woman caught committing adultery was brought to Jesus. 'This woman was taken in adultery,' the plaintiffs said. 'Our law commands us to stone such a woman. What have you to say about her?' Jesus did not answer, but wrote something on the ground. When the woman's condemners pressed the question, Jesus faced them and said, 'If any one of you is without sin, let him be the first to throw a stone at her' (John 8:7). And again he stooped down, and wrote on the ground. All in the crowd were convicted by their consciences. Ashamed of their own sins, they said nothing more, and disappeared 'one at a time, the older ones first, until only Jesus was left' (v 9).

A Japanese poet declares:

You say, 'I have no sin'
But if you ask your heart
You know it's perjury.
To see one's heart reflected
In the mirror's glass,
How ugly it must be!

If we stop dealing with other people's sins and start examining ourselves we will come to know how sinful we really are. The purest person is the one who fully and sorrowfully acknowledges the sin in his heart. A person's uprightness can be judged by the sincerity of his repentance for sin. Confucius lamented: 'I am not virtuous. I cannot study much. I hear what is right, but I cannot put it into practice. I cannot correct my unrighteousness. I grieve over this.'

The apostle Paul also grieved: 'For what I do is not the good I want to do; no, the evil I do not want to do – this I keep on doing' (Romans 7:19). 'Christ Jesus came into the world to save sinners – of whom I am the worst' (1 Timothy 1:15). 'When Simon Peter saw this, he fell at Jesus' knees and said, "Go away from me, Lord; I am a sinful man!"' (Luke 5:8). It is said that Martin Luther shut himself away in a cell, so profoundly did he realise and regret his sin.

Some hundreds of years ago in Italy there was a very religious man named Ginepro. Worried about his sins, he walked the streets dressed like a beggar. At the time, the district was governed by an evil and lawless man who was hated by the people. There was a rumour abroad that someone was plotting to take his life and that the assassin would be camouflaged as a beggar. Because of this, the religious man was arrested, brought to court and tried.

'What are you?' he was asked.

'I am a grievous sinner,' he replied.

'What sins have you committed?' asked the prosecutor.

'I am a rebel,' the man answered, 'and I am not worthy of God's blessing.'

'Have you plotted to kill the governor?'

'Oh, worse than that; I have sinned against God himself.'

The man was sentenced to death. On his way to the place of execution he met one of his friends who intervened to save his life. The friend explained to the authorities that Ginepro was innocent of any plot against the governor's life and would never violate any law. Ginepro's concern was not to violate divine grace. The story may be exaggerated, but it is a pointed illustration of how deeply the sincere person repents of his sin. All are sinners in God's sight, and we should be ashamed of our sins. All sin must be hated.

'The fool says in his heart, "There is no God." They are corrupt, their deeds are vile; there is no one who does good. The LORD looks down from Heaven on the sons of men to see if there are any who understand, any who seek God. All have turned aside, they have together become corrupt; there is no one who does good, not even one. Will evildoers never learn – those who devour my people as men eat bread and who do not call on the LORD? There they are, overwhelmed with dread, for God is present in the company of the righteous' (Psalm 14:1-5).

Sin is the source of all misfortune

'We might be able to avoid natural disasters,' said the ancients, 'but it is impossible to avoid those disasters which result from one's own deeds.' We may have to suffer because of flood or fire, robbery or sickness, or even storms and earthquakes. But the worst of all disasters results from our sins. Before God all are sinners, and all suffer as a result of sin. 'Woe unto them who make falsehood a cord, and with it pull evil as a wheel is pulled by a rope.'

Sin affects the body

British Prime Minister William Gladstone said disasters caused by alcohol are beyond those caused by war, epidemic and famine. King Solomon rebuked the men of misconduct, reminding them that a man can be reduced to poverty by an evil woman, and even lose their lives because of her. 'Her house is a highway to the grave, leading down to the chambers of death' (Proverbs 7:27). 'But a man who commits adultery lacks judgement; whoever does so destroys himself. Blows and disgrace are his lot, and his shame will never be wiped away' (Proverbs 6:32, 33).

Convicts in Sugamo Prison wrote: 'We pursued red kimonos [worn by prostitutes] and now we suffer in red prison uniforms.' Satan often uses two giant snares to trap men – alcoholism and immorality.

It is said that US President Benjamin Franklin once observed that if the people were ordered to work for the government one-tenth of their time they would consider it a severe imposition. But laziness demands a much heavier tax. The lazy man becomes ill and dies in his youth. Laziness is like rust. When rusty metal is cleaned on a grindstone, the rust takes with it some of the essential metal.

'The fox which rises late never catches the bird,' declares a Japanese proverb. If a man rises at a late hour, he chases his business throughout the whole day. He cannot catch up with it. Even in the evenings he is still pursuing it. 'Poverty runs so fast that laziness cannot catch up with it,' another proverb declares, and yet another states: 'The lazy man who does nothing but wait for good fortune to arrive will soon starve.' A proportion of the poverty, famine and difficulty in the world is the result of laziness, misconduct and unbelief, and sickness is sometimes caused by intemperance and misconduct.

Sin affects the heart

Wicked people know no peace of heart. Always the sinner has a guilty conscience, with which it is difficult to live. A man named Wine went into a draper's shop in London. He killed the owner and the owner's wife, stole a great deal of drapery and fled to America. Skillfully he evaded detection. A suspect, however, was arrested and charged with the robbery. The man had no alibi and was executed. Wine spent 20 years in America, happy with his wife and children, and became very rich. He then returned to London for a visit. As Wine came out of a shop he saw a policeman chasing a thief and shouting, 'Catch him. Catch that man!' Wine felt so convicted of the sin he had committed 20 years before that he confessed there and then to the policeman.

God exposes the secret sins of men. Man cannot hide anything from God. It is good to live honestly and without blame; it is abhorrent to live untruthfully. Sinners cannot enjoy peace in their heart.

Sin determines the soul's destiny

The soul of man lives on after death, but God, being all-righteous, can accept into Heaven only souls without sin. When a sinner dies, because of his sin he must go to Hell. Those who live self-centred lives against God's will cannot remain in his presence. Jesus said: 'If your hand or your foot causes you to sin, cut it off and throw it away. It is better for you to enter life maimed or crippled than to have two hands or two feet and be thrown into eternal fire. And if your eye causes you to sin, gouge it out and throw it away. It is better for you to enter life with one eye than to have two eyes and be thrown into the fire of Hell' (Matthew 18:8, 9).

'There was a rich man who was dressed in purple and fine linen and lived in luxury every day. At his gate was laid a beggar named Lazarus, covered with sores and longing to eat what fell from the rich man's table. Even the dogs came and licked his sores. The time came when the beggar died and the angels carried him to Abraham's side. The rich man also died and was buried. In Hell, where he was in torment, he looked up and saw Abraham far away, with Lazarus by his side. So he called to him, "Father Abraham, have pity on me and send Lazarus to dip the tip of his finger in water and cool my tongue, because I am in agony in this fire." But Abraham replied, "Son, remember that in your lifetime you received your good things, while Lazarus received bad things, but now he is comforted here and you are in agony. And besides all this, between us and you a great chasm has been fixed, so that those who want to go from here to you cannot, nor can anyone cross over from there to us." He answered, "Then I beg you, father, send Lazarus to my father's house, for I have five brothers. Let him warn them, so that they will not also come to this place of torment." Abraham replied, "They have Moses and the Prophets, let them listen to them." "No, father Abraham," he said, "but if someone from the dead goes to them, they will repent." He said to him "If they do not listen to Moses and the Prophets, they will not be convinced even if someone rises from the dead.'" (Luke 16:19-31).

Sin multiplies

Sin is man's most dreaded enemy. It is the subtle foe that torments men on earth, and after death consigns them to hell. Sin has the demonic power to increase itself. One sin becomes many. The sinner makes friends of other sinners and becomes part of an evil group of men. Sin is like a snowball. As it is rolled along it gets bigger and bigger. It is like a bacillus during an epidemic. It spreads its poison widely.

A Western proverb says Satan uses four phrases to lead men into sin: 'Everyone does it,' 'It's only a small thing,' 'You can try it once' and 'Time is on your side.'

A Japanese proverb states: 'A man drinks the first glass of sake [a Japanese alcoholic drink]. Sake drinks the second glass of sake. Sake drinks the man in the third glass of sake.' Both proverbs warn us that Satan takes advantage of the careless man and leads him from a small sin to larger sins. Just as the sleeve of a kimono gathers dust in its folds, so sin increases without our being aware of it. A Japanese song says, 'If you don't want to get wet, you must not touch even a dewdrop.' The man who commits the smallest sin can be led by it to the commission of desperate, horrible sins.

In a small town on Shikoku Island several young people decided to have some fun by threatening a notorious miser. They armed themselves with fake swords and, menacingly, entered the miser's house. 'If you won't give us money we will kill you,' they shouted. The miser trembled and begged for his life, not understanding that the whole thing was a hoax.

He offered the youths money which they accepted, and which they quickly spent in eating and drinking. It had all been so simple, and the consequences so enjoyable, that the youths could not stop robbing people. Before long they were confirmed thieves. If we imitate wrongdoing, it becomes actual wrongdoing. How conscientious we should be!

A notorious robber, Goemon Ishikawa, was sentenced to death, with his son. In distress, he cried out, 'The source of robbery is the lie. The source of the lie is misbehaviour. Once young people begin to do wrong, their hands move by themselves and they take what does not belong to them. Next they make evil friends. They find they cannot stop their thievery. The wheel rolls ever faster, by itself, down the slope. Now, it is too late for me to repent. Not only I, but my son also, must suffer. How sad! I am ashamed of the life I have lived. When a bird is dying, it is said, it chirps sadly. When a man is dying, his words are honest.'

Goemon Ishikawa's statement confirms that sin multiplies rapidly from a tiny beginning and speedily carries a man far astray. Alas, the sinner's sins affect not only himself but others too.

An impure heart turns an innocent man into a sinner who can upset an entire community and pain the heart of God. We should be afraid of sin's propensity to multiply and affect others – friends, relatives, descendants. All too often the sinner is imitated. The Geisha girl who mimics an actor will be imitated by the wives and daughters of decent families.

Many years ago, a creator of earthenware named Botcher was dissatisfied with one of his productions and tried to drown his disappointment by drinking sake. Those who worked for him usually followed his example, so it became the custom of the factory workers to drink more and more sake until they were quarrelling among themselves from morning to night without accomplishing any work. Finally, the government sent in a troop of soldiers who arrested 300 workers and took them to prison. One man's sin can lead many others into evil ways.

A man's sin can also affect his descendants. Years ago a baby girl was born in Germany. When she grew up she became a chronic drunkard, became homeless, and died at 60 years of age. Professor Berman examined the life of this woman, Ada York, and learned something of the power of sin to affect others. Ada York, according to the study, had 834 descendants over almost two centuries. The professor could only review 709 of them, but among that number there were 109 illegitimate children, 142 beggars, 64 who were indigent in almshouses, 181 prostitutes, 76 criminals and seven murderers. The cost of caring for these unfortunates in prison, hospital and almshouse was enormous. One person's sin can frighteningly affect his or her descendants.

'You shall have no other gods before me. You shall not make for yourself an idol in the form of anything in Heaven above or on the earth beneath or in the waters below. You shall not bow down to them or worship them; for I, the LORD your God, am a jealous God, punishing the children for the sin of the fathers to the third and fourth generation of those who hate me, but showing love to a thousand generations of those who love me and keep my commandments' (Exodus 20:3-6).

Man cannot save himself

I have already written about the horrible results of sin, and everyone should do their best to avoid sinning. Rules have been made and laws enacted to stop people from wrongdoing, but without success. A man's sin resides deeply in his heart. He may pluck off the leaves of his words and the fruit of his conduct, but the sin has the power to produce again the same leaves and fruit. The law, discipline, rebuke, disinheritance, or one's own decision, cannot save men from the power of sin. The Bible says, 'Then, after desire has conceived, it gives birth to sin; and sin, when it is full-grown, gives birth to death' (James 1:15). That is how man falls into destruction's trap. 'For sin, seizing the opportunity afforded by the commandment, deceived me, and through the commandment put me to death' (Romans 7:11). Rules and regulations have no power to save men. Sometimes they push men from one evil to another – to commit further sin in order to cover up the first sin.

'It is easy to destroy the burglars in the mountain,' a Chinese governor once lamented, 'but it is difficult to destroy the burglar in one's heart.' A Russian emperor came to the same conclusion: 'I know how to govern the Russian nation, but I can't govern my own heart.' Similar statements have been made by Japanese poets: 'The heart deludes the heart, but we should not allow it' and 'Even if I make up my mind, I change it often. I cannot trust my own mind.'

Yukichi Fukuzawa was a wise man of the Meiji era. In his autobiography he confessed to the use of tobacco and sake. 'I have suffered greatly because of sake. When I was a student in a private school I thought that drinking sake was harmful, and I decided not to indulge. My friends laughed at me, saying, "Fukuzawa has stopped drinking. How long can he bear it? He won't last 10 days. In fact, he will start drinking after three days." I abstained for more than half a month, and my intimate friends told me, "You are very determined. We are amazed that you have abstained for so long. But perhaps it is unwise to prohibit a habit so suddenly, even if the habit is an undesirable one. You would be wise to start having another habit, seeing we can't live without any pleasures at all." So I started to smoke tobacco, even though I hated it. Previously, I was the one who used to challenge my friends by asking them, "Why do you smoke? It is a useless habit, and unclean. Even the smell of tobacco offends me. Please don't smoke in my presence." In view of this it was strange that I should begin to smoke; but when I thought of my friends' opinion it seemed right and reasonable. My friends were generous. They lent me pipes and gave me tobacco. Some even bought a special kind of tobacco for me to smoke. But they were not really kind to me. Now they got together to laugh at me – the one who had reprimanded them for smoking!

'Because I was eager not to drink, I smoked excessively. At first I disliked it, but the habit grew on me. After one month I was an habitual smoker. But now I found I could not forget the taste of sake. I know I deceived myself, but one day I took just a sip of sake. How tasty it was! I didn't want to take any more, but I couldn't stop. I decided that once the bottle was empty there would be no more drinking. But again I couldn't stop, and soon I was drinking as much as before. After a month I was both a chronic drinker and smoker. I am now over 60 years of age and have stopped drinking. But I still smoke, even though it is not good for one's health. The loss is mine. I have no words of excuse.'

We cannot overcome the domination of sake and tobacco by will power alone. Likewise, it is exceedingly difficult for a person to overcome pride, lying, greed, lust, infidelity, laziness, jealousy, thievery, unkindness, unbelief, and so on. There are false moralists who, outwardly, live circumspect lives but who, unknown to others, act immorally in the house of the prostitute. These are they whom Jesus called 'whitewashed tombs' (Matthew 23:27). The exterior may be splendid, but within there are skeletons and corruption. They are unworthy objects in the sight of a God who sees and knows all.

What then can we do? Surely it is better to be honest and sincere rather than try to cover up our sins with lying excuses. There is no other way for us to be saved from our sins but to open our heart and show God what we really are. When we do this, we can rely on God to save us by his power, as he did for King David who offered this prayer of repentance:

'Have mercy on me, O God, according to your unfailing love; according to your great compassion blot out my transgressions. Wash away all my iniquity and cleanse me from my sin. For I know my transgressions, and my sin is always before me. Against you, you only, have I sinned and done what is evil in your sight, so that you are proved right when you speak and justified when you judge. Surely I was sinful at birth, sinful from the time my mother conceived me. Surely you desire truth in the inner parts; you teach me wisdom in the inmost place. Cleanse me with hyssop, and I shall be clean; wash me, and I shall be whiter than snow. Let me hear joy and gladness; let the bones you have crushed rejoice. Hide your face from my sins and blot out all my iniquity. Create in me a pure heart, O God, and renew a steadfast spirit within me. Do not cast me from your presence or take your Holy

Spirit from me. Restore to me the joy of your salvation and grant me a willing spirit, to sustain me' (Psalm 51:1-12).

Repent and return to a Heavenly Father

Sin is the most horrible, hateful, shameful thing in the world. Man, however, cannot save himself from his own sins. There is only one way of salvation – by confessing all one's past sins to the Heavenly Father who, by his grace and power, will change our miserable lives for the better. To repent of sin is the first step towards belief in the only true God.

Jesus told this parable. A man had two sons. The younger son asked the father to give him his share of the inheritance. The father divided the inheritance and gave half to each son. The younger son immediately left home and went to a far country. There he led a dissipated life and lost everything. Then came a serious famine. The young man who was used to being treated as a rich person had nothing to eat. His hair became dishevelled. His clothes were torn. The only work he could get was tending pigs, and since he could not get enough to eat, he at last ate what the pigs were fed.

He finally came to himself and admitted that he had been an undutiful son, lacking in gratitude, and that he had spent his substance in riotous living. He realised that at home even his father's employees would have enough to eat and to spare, while he was wandering in a foreign country almost dying of starvation. All this was because he had gone against his father's will and obstinately followed his own. Where and what he was, was his own fault. There was no one to blame but himself. What should he do? Should he die in the gutter? No, he would return home and seek his father's forgiveness.

In his weakness he staggered home. So great was the father's love that he did not reprimand the erring son. He hugged him closely and rejoiced over his repentance. 'I thought he had died,' said the father, 'but now he is alive. I thought he was lost, but now he is found. I can know no greater joy than this.' Then the father gave him new clothes and celebrated the son's return with a great banquet.

The parable makes it plain that God is a merciful Father, and that the prodigal son is the one who leaves God to wander in the ways of destruction and who repeatedly commits sin. Those who commit sin and suffer its disastrous results have no power to redeem themselves. Thankfully, a forgiving Heavenly Father has prepared a way of salvation for us. When we appeal to him, he forgives our sin, cleanses our heart and strengthens us against failing again into error.

Only the grace of God can save man from his sin and its punishment. In order to merit this grace there must be repentance and faith. A long time ago a thinker observed that the bitter persimmon tree is ungrateful to the farmer who for eight or nine years carefully tends the tree only to find that the fruit it produces is not sweet. Like the tree, we are kept by the rich grace of God, but we commit sin and wound the heart of God. We are the astringent persimmon in God's garden.

A Japanese proverb provides an analogy: 'Before a sour persimmon is skewered, even a crow would refuse to eat it. But once the fruit is peeled and skewered and dried in the sun, it becomes delightful to the taste.' Similarly, if a man's soul is pierced with the skewer of repentance, his evil words and deeds peeled away, and his heart exposed to the light of God's grace, then he will become a completely changed individual. He will be a saved man, speaking truth and doing good deeds. To repent of one's sins is the first condition in accepting the grace of God.

The German Chancellor, Prince Otto Bismarck, was ill and called for a doctor. While the doctor was examining him he asked the Iron Chancellor certain questions. Because Bismarck would not answer, the doctor become angry. 'If you don't want to tell me, your doctor, about your symptoms, it is useless for me to continue the examination. You had better call in a veterinary surgeon to help you!' If we want spiritual healing and forgiveness, it is necessary for us to confess the sickness of our heart, and to repent of all our sins before God.

'Now there were some present at that time who told Jesus about the Galileans whose blood Pilate had mixed with their sacrifices. Jesus answered, "Do you think that these Galileans were worse sinners than all the other Galileans because they suffered this way? I tell you, no! But unless you repent, you too will all perish. Or those eighteen who died when the tower in Siloam fell on them – do you think they were more guilty than all the others living in Jerusalem? I tell you, no! But unless you repent, you too will all perish." Then he told this parable: "A man had a fig-tree, planted in his vineyard, and he went to look for fruit on it, but did not find any. So he said to the man who took care of the vineyard, 'For three years now I've been coming to look for fruit on this fig-tree and haven't found any. Cut it down! Why should it use up the soil?' 'Sir,' the man replied, 'leave it alone for one more year, and I'll dig round it and fertilise it. If it bears fruit next year, fine! If not, then cut it down.'" (Luke 13:1-9).

Three

Salvation through Christ

Jesus Christ is the Son of God
Mr Hongo, a government official, founded a home for orphans, and did his best to care for them. He sent them into the streets to work as shoeblacks, but the venture was a failure. The children were too young to work diligently on their own. All day long they played, stopping only to eat their lunch. If they did earn any money, they spent it. One night, Mr Hongo overheard the children talking. One asked, 'What do you want to be when you grow up?' Another said, 'I'm fed up working as a shoeblack. Mr Hongo has a good job, in an office, and I want to be like him, a government official.'

Mr Hongo felt as though he had been struck by lightning. 'I must take the blame,' he thought. 'Every morning I dress in smart clothes and go to the office while the children go out into the streets in shabby clothing to work at a most menial task. How can I possibly bring them up properly if this goes on?'

The next morning he resigned his government position. He put on old clothes and an old cap on which he wrote: 'Five pence for small shoes. Eight pence for large shoes,' and went out with the children shouting, 'Shoeblack, shoeblack.' Following his example, the children worked hard and profitably. Their training become easier because of Mr Hongo's example, companionship and encouragement.

Mr Richard, an authority on the education of mentally disabled people, one day watched a mother observing her disabled child making mischief in the garden. The woman didn't shout at the boy or scold him. Instead, she went into the garden and spoke softly to the child, telling him quietly that what he was doing was wrong. In that incident, Mr Richard said, he discovered the secret of successful teaching.

Catherine Booth, one of the Founders of The Salvation Army, when she was 12 years of age, saw a drunk man being taken to the police station. People were shouting at the man and cursing him. Catherine wanted him to know he had a friend, so she took the prisoner's hand and walked with him to the police station.

The great educationalist, Johann Heinrich Pestalozzi, once said, 'I live like a beggar in order to save the child of a beggar.' The man who would save the outcast must walk with him. If he wants to save the beggar, he must become the friend of the beggar. That is why the Son of God left his place in Heaven and came to earth in the form of a man, so he might save us from our sins.

Jesus is the only Son of God, but he came to earth 2,000 years ago. He was born in the country of Judea, and worked as a carpenter in the village of Nazareth. He made chairs. He laid floors. He worked hard. When he became 30 years of age he revealed his divine mission to the world. He healed the sick, comforted the suffering and taught the people that God is our Heavenly Father. He reminded his hearers that though they were God's children, they often forgot him and strayed into the world of sin. They should repent of their wrongdoing and return to God.

When he was 33 he was taken by wicked men and crucified. He died as the Substitute for all sinners. 'Very rarely will anyone die for a righteous man, though for a good man someone might possibly dare to die. But God demonstrates his own love for us in this: While we were still sinners, Christ died for us' (Romans 5:7, 8). The infinite love of God is clearly revealed in the fact that he sent his only Son into this world to save us.

Of course, even before Christ came, there were philosophers who thought about God and taught people how they should live. Their views and their teachings, however, were not based on certain knowledge. One might look through a doorway into a house and say: 'There are shoes here, and I can hear someone coughing. Someone must live in this house. The room beyond appears in good order, so the occupant must be a tidy person. The name-plate on the door is done in excellent brushwriting, so the one who lives here must be competent in reading and writing.'

In the same way, when wise men observed the organisation and structure of the created world, they could speculate about its Creator, and could perhaps guess that God is omnipotent and merciful. But despite such deductions, something was still missing. To the man looking through the doorway of the house, the owner was unrevealed and therefore unknown.

When Jesus Christ, the Son of God, came into the world, it meant that the Son of the Master of the house came out through the doorway and spoke to the people at the gate. To them he explained everything about the Master – his views, his business, his interests. No longer was it the suppositions of wise men and scholars. Now, it was an intimate revelation by a member of God's family. Because of it, men could now understand the way of true faith and know their spiritual duty. Jesus declared: 'Anyone who has seen me has seen the Father' (John 14:9). And he taught: 'Everyone who hears these words of mine and puts them into practice is like a wise man who built his house on the rock' (Matthew 7:24).

The greatest treasure a man can have is faith in the Son of God, Jesus Christ. It is the only solid foundation on which he can build his life. 'Your attitude should be the same as that of Christ Jesus:

Who, being in very nature God, did not consider equality with God something to be grasped, but made himself nothing, taking the very nature of a servant, being made in human likeness. And being found in appearance as a man, he humbled himself and became obedient to death – even death on a cross! Therefore God exalted him to the highest place and gave him the name that is above every name, that at the name of Jesus every knee should bow, in heaven and on earth and under the earth, and every tongue confess that Jesus Christ is Lord, to the glory of God the Father' (Philippians 2:5-11).

Christ is the Saviour of all mankind

Jesus Christ, the Son of God, died on a cross to save us from our sins. Let me explain. As I have already written, all men should repent of their sins and return to God. But how can we cancel out those past sins over which we have already repented? Can we obliterate them simply by thereafter living sinless lives? The answer is no.

For example, a man goes to a shop and buys goods. He promises to pay for them at the end of the month. When the end of the month comes, can he say to the shopkeeper, 'I'll pay cash for next month's supply of goods, but please forget about the goods I took away last month?' Would the merchant say, 'That's quite all right'? It is normal that the man should pay cash for his future purchases, but if the man does not pay the existing debt, how can the merchant forgive him? It should be normal for us to do good, but we cannot make up for past sins by future goodness. How then can our past sins be cancelled?

A Japanese legend says people used to give some of their personal effects as an offering for sin. They went to the riverside, or to the seashore, put the belongings on a raft, prayed to their god, and then set the raft afloat. The number of rafts indicated the number of their sins. One man might float four rafts, another eight. It is said that one man had to float 1,000 rafts in order to rid himself of the sins he had committed against his parents and his elder sister. To persuade his god to forgive such sins the man also shaved off his beard and pulled out his fingernails.

In more recent times there have been those who hoped to expiate their past sins by building temples or shrines, or by giving alms to the poor.

God's love for all mankind, as revealed in the life and death of Jesus, was manifested first in the country of Judea. But just as a farmer transplants the rice seedlings from the nursery to the paddy field, so God conveyed the way of truth to all the world. In Judea, when atoning for sin, the custom was to sacrifice an ox or a lamb to God. The people, symbolically, laid their sins upon the animal, with the prayer that their transgressions would be forgiven. But when the way of salvation through Christ, the Son of God, was revealed, such ceremonies gradually disappeared. 'But when perfection comes, the imperfect disappears' (1 Corinthians 13:10).

Those who put Christ to death were wicked men who thought themselves virtuous. Then why did not Christ, who was himself the Son of God, flee from the cross? Why did he die there so ignominiously?

The reason is that, amazingly, he wanted to become the Sacrifice for the sins of all humanity. In offering his sinless life on the cross he bore the iniquity of all. No matter how vile the sinner, if the sinner repents of his sin and believes that Christ died in his place, and exercises faith in God, he will be forgiven and transformed by grace into a man with a clean heart.

The Bible emphasises this truth. 'For God so loved the world that he gave his one and only Son, that whoever believes in him shall not perish but have eternal life' (John 3:16). 'For you know that it was not with perishable things such as silver or gold that you were redeemed from the empty way of life handed down to you from your forefathers, but with the precious blood of Christ, a lamb without blemish or defect' (1 Peter 1:18, 19). Hallelujah!

Many years ago, Sogoro Sakura was put to death on a cross in order to save the inhabitants of 229 Japanese villages from the oppression of a feudal lord. Jesus Christ, the Son of God, died on a cross to save all mankind from sin and destruction. If people were impressed by the sacrificial deed of Sogoro

Sakura, and were grateful to him, how much more should men accept the love of Christ in gratitude and faith!

When the Emperor of France Napoleon Bonaparte was campaigning against a foreign army, a son of the manor was conscripted as a soldier. In accordance with custom, the high-born youth asked another young man to go to the battlefront in his place, while he remained at home to manage the family's affairs. One day, news came that the substitute soldier had died on the battlefield. Twelve years later, Napoleon again summoned the young men of the country to his side, and a government official came to the young scion with the order.

'Twelve years ago,' said the young man, 'I sent my substitute to the battlefield. He died there. That means that I died there. Surely it is not reasonable to ask a dead man to fight again.'

'But you are alive now,' argued the official, to no avail. Finally, an appeal was made to Napoleon himself who decreed that, by substitution, the young man had already given his life for his country and so was exempted from further military service.

Those who believe that Christ, as their Substitute, died on the cross for their sins are forgiven. They are regarded as never having sinned at all. Condemnation and remorse disappear. By grace they become the children of God, able to enter into his presence at any time. Hallelujah! How wonderful is the grace of our Saviour Christ!

'But now a righteousness from God, apart from law, has been made known, to which the Law and the Prophets testify. This righteousness from God comes through faith in Jesus Christ to all who believe. There is no difference, for all have sinned and fall short of the glory of God, and are justified freely by his grace through the redemption that came by Christ Jesus. God presented him as a sacrifice of atonement, through faith in his blood. He did this to demonstrate his justice, because in his forbearance he had left the sins committed beforehand unpunished – he did it to demonstrate his justice at the present time, so as to be just and the one who justifies those who have faith in Jesus' (Romans 3:21-26).

Behold, now is the day of salvation

The first message given by Jesus was, 'Repent, and believe the gospel.' The apostle Paul, who took the gospel to Asia, carried with him the same exhortation: 'Repent before God, and believe in Jesus.' The way to receive forgiveness for sin is, first, to repent of all wrongdoing and, second, to have faith in Jesus Christ. These are the two wheels of a cart, the two wings of a bird. If a man returns to God in repentance and faith, God forgives his sins and bestows the gift of salvation.

As a tax gatherer Zacchaeus became rich, but he repented of his sins and made up his mind to repay fourfold all he had gained unjustly, and to put his trust in Jesus. Christ was moved by Zacchaeus's good intentions and said, 'Today salvation has come to this house' (Luke 19:9).

One of the robbers crucified with Jesus, his hands and feet nailed to a cross, and on the point of expiring, repented. 'Please save my soul,' he pleaded with Jesus. The answer came at once, 'Today you will be with me in paradise.'

Scripture says, 'For he says, "In the time of my favour I heard you, and in the day of salvation I helped you." I tell you, now is the time of God's favour, now is the day of salvation' (2 Corinthians 6:2). If you repent of your sins and have faith in Jesus Christ, you can be saved from all your sins – now, instantaneously. If you, dear reader, have not yet accepted salvation through Christ, let me suggest that when you finish reading this paragraph, you close the book, and kneel down just where you are, and pray to our Heavenly Father. It will not be difficult. Come before God with a humble heart, as a little child would come to his parents, and pray in the following words: 'Heavenly Father, I am a sinner. But I have heard that you save those who repent of their sins and have faith in your Son, Jesus Christ. I now confess my sins and sincerely repent of them, and I believe that Jesus saves me. Please keep me from sin and by your grace make me a new person. Amen.'

It is enough. If a prayer like this is offered humbly and sincerely, God forgives. It is not necessary to go on repeating prayers of repentance. Feeling does not matter. It is faith that is vital. And if you make up your mind to live according to God's will, he will help you because you are now one of his children. Hallelujah! Keep on believing. Read the Bible. Seek to know the will of God for your life. Pray continually and follow the counsels of God. Live your life with him. You will discover that your thoughts, your speech, your behaviour have completely changed following your conversion.

There are two small lakes high in the Canadian Rockies. They are not far from each other and are on the same level. But there is a vast difference in the destinations towards which the waters of the two lakes flow. One stream proceeds eastwards into the Mississippi River and ends in the Gulf of Mexico. The other flows westwards and becomes the Columbia River which empties into the Pacific Ocean. The sources of the two rivers are close; their destinations far apart. When a man repents of his sins and exercises faith in Christ, his destination is decided. He moves towards life instead of death, to Heaven rather than Hell, to victory rather than failure.

On his deathbed a man said, 'When I was young I had the opportunity to believe in Christ as my Saviour, but I listened instead to the voice of Satan and delayed making the decision. When I reached middle-age I still delayed. Now I am very old. I have no god, no hope, and face the destruction of hell.' He died in an agony of spirit. Confucius said, 'If a man knows what is right and does not do it, it is because he lacks courage.' Takamori Saigo felt this to be so. 'Delay and doubt,' he said, 'is proof that one lacks sincerity.' My desire is that every reader will accept the blessing of salvation, and that no one will come to such a miserable end as the man to whom I have just made reference.

'Then Moses said, "You have been set apart to the LORD today, for you were against your own sons and brothers, and he has blessed you this day."' (Exodus 32:29).

'See to it, brothers, that none of you has a sinful, unbelieving heart that turns away from the living God. But encourage one another daily, as long as it is called Today, so that none of you may be hardened by sin's deceitfulness. We have come to share in Christ if we hold firmly till the end of the confidence we had at first. As has just been said: "Today, if you hear his voice, do not harden your hearts as you did in the rebellion." Who were they who heard and rebelled? Were they not all those Moses led out of Egypt? And with whom was he angry for forty years? Was it not with those who sinned, whose bodies fell in the desert? And to whom did God swear that they would never enter his rest if not to those who disobeyed? So we see that they were not able to enter, because of their unbelief' (Hebrews 3:12-19).

That which is born of the Spirit is spirit
The first blessing God gives to the person who has repented of his sin and exercised faith for salvation is the forgiveness of sin. The second blessing is the new birth of the soul.

An Indian Salvationist went to France, and with French Salvationists marched through the streets. A policeman thought it was a Frenchman dressed up and arrested him for posturing as an Indian. At the police station the man was ordered to wash his face. He did so, but his complexion remained the same. The policeman then realised that the man really was an Indian, and released him. The Bible says, 'Can the Ethiopian change his skin or the leopard its spots? Neither can you do good who are accustomed to doing evil' (Jeremiah 13:23). Sin is associated with man just as is the colour of the skin to the Indian or the Ethiopian, and just as the spots on the skin belong to the leopard. Sin seems natural to man, and he is powerless to escape from it in his own strength.

A newspaper article told of a government official who made up his mind to stop drinking sake. He went with his friends to a drugstore to buy medicine that would take away his taste for the wine. When they arrived at the pharmacy, they all hesitated to enter. 'You go,' said one. 'No, you go first,' said another. They spent so much time debating the issue that finally someone said, 'Oh, let's go and have a drink.' And that is just what they did.

A European government once prohibited the sale of alcoholic beverages. Those who were chronic drinkers began to visit other countries to buy liquor. Those who had been used to taking only a small drink before retiring, now, finding themselves away from home, drank long and hard throughout the day. All sorts of complications arose, medically and economically, in their lives. The Bible explains such excesses by stating: 'For the sinful nature desires what is contrary to the Spirit, and the Spirit what is contrary to the sinful nature. They are in conflict with each other, so that you do not do what you want' (Galatians 5:17).

God, however, can give the soul of man a new birth. He not only forgives the sins of those who repent and have faith in Christ, but also brings the soul to new life by the Spirit. The blood of Christ atones for our sins, and by the power of the Spirit the soul is reborn. When we receive these two blessings we are truly saved. The newborn person hates sin and longs for righteousness. Now, he does not serve Satan, but follows God. He does not plan selfishly; his conduct becomes pure. Before conversion he thought only of bad things and did bad things. Now, he thinks of good things and does good things. His heart is completely changed. This is the wonderful work of the Spirit of God in the heart of a man.

A man named Müller stole when young, and was imprisoned. Changed by Christ, he became an unusually good man and spent his life caring for orphans, some 120,000 of whom he sheltered in his lifetime.

Jo Niijima was an ambitious student who went to America. He wrote a song which declared, 'A soldier's decision is very strong. Once he makes up his mind, he will not return home without glory.' After 10 years' study he wrote another song: 'The glory with which I return is in a box. It is not yet the time for me to show it to the people.' He returned to Kyoto, where he preached the gospel despite suffering misunderstanding and persecution, and sought to train young people in the Christian way of life.

Kamekichi Watanabe was put into prison at 15 years of age for pickpocketing. Seven further incarcerations followed, and at the age of 19 he was sentenced to 10 years of penal servitude. He was converted and become a completely new person. He studied diligently, so diligently that he lost the sight of one eye. Having learned to read, he made every effort to preach the gospel to prisoners and orphans. The last 15 years of his life were devoted to this work.

An evangelist once asked Methodist preacher John Summerfield, 'Where is your birthplace?'

'Liverpool and Dublin,' he replied.

'How can you have two birthplaces,' he was asked.

'Can't you understand?' said Summerfield, 'you are an evangelist, aren't you? You should know that my body was born in Liverpool and my soul in Dublin.'

'Flesh gives birth to flesh, but the Spirit gives birth to spirit' (John 3:6). Dear reader: you should seek this precious experience of the soul's rebirth with God's help, now!

'Now there was a man of the Pharisees named Nicodemus, a member of the Jewish ruling council. He came to Jesus at night and said, "Rabbi, we know you are a teacher who has come from God. For no one could perform the miraculous signs and are doing if God were not with him. In reply Jesus declared, "I tell you the truth, no one can see the kingdom of God unless he is born again" "How can a man be born when he is old?" Nicodemus asked. "Surely he cannot enter a second time into his mother's womb to be born!" Jesus answered, "I tell you the truth, no one can enter the kingdom of God unless he is born of water and the Spirit. Flesh gives birth to flesh, but the Spirit gives birth to spirit. You should not be surprised at my saying, "You must be born again." The wind blows wherever it pleases. You hear its sound, but you cannot tell where it comes from or where it is going. So it is with everyone born of the Spirit"' (John 3:1-8).

The religion of Christ is the religion of victory

The blessing of salvation was once explained by a Chinese person like this: 'I was travelling the path of life but fell into a deep well of sin and agony. I knew that if I did not escape I would die, so I shouted for help. By chance, Buddha came and looked down at me. "Poor soul," he said, "you are in the well because of what the generations before you have done. Think about the law of causality and resign yourself to death." He left, and I again shouted for help. Along came Confucius. He also looked down at me and said, "If a man is careless he falls, as you did. You should be more careful the next time, and not fall into the well again." He then went away. Just then, Jesus Christ came running to the well. He brought a long ladder and climbed down it to the bottom of the well. He helped me to get up out of the well, gave me medicine, bandaged my wounds and kindly cared for me. When I recovered, he explained what was wrong with me, and gave me some good guidance for my future. He sent me on my happy way to Heaven.'

As in this illustration, Jesus, the Son of God, come down to earth, took the figure of a man, experienced all sorts of hardship and was finally crucified in an act of atonement for our sins. Through his Spirit he gave men the gift of a new birth. He is the true Saviour. Hallelujah!

One of the first results of this salvation from sin and the rebirth of the soul is our reconciliation with God, our Heavenly Father, whose child we become. It is a lovely thing to see a parent and a child smiling at each other. If something makes us happy, we can share it with our Heavenly Father. If something worries us, we can speak to God about it. Our whole life can be shared with him.

A French Christian named Teresa, who had only one silver coin, established an orphanage. 'For Teresa to have only one silver coin is nothing,' she said. 'But God and a silver coin can move the world.'

When we are saved and know God as our Heavenly Father, we need be afraid of nothing, no matter how weak we are within ourselves. We can stamp out sin, Satan and lust, and work for God as we should. I would like to illustrate this by reporting on a 'Satan's funeral' conducted in one Salvation Army corps.

Burying Satan

The religion of Jesus Christ is the religion of victory. It is the religion that overcomes Satan, worldliness and lust. Believers can be more than conquerors over trouble, persecution, hunger, arrest and the sword. Praise God!

Kanda Corps had a special meeting entitled, 'The Funeral of Satan'. During the ceremony we buried many things which had been captured from Satan's territory while fighting the good fight of faith. First, the smokers' pipes. While under the domination of Satan they were considered treasures, and we could not part with them. Now, we bury them; they are not hygienic, but harmful and uneconomical. The congregation was asked if anyone present wanted to make the same decision. A young boy offered his pipe and asked that it be buried. Hallelujah! We prayed that God would keep this boy and help him to stand by his decision all through his life.

The next item to be buried was a pack of cards. Several years ago a book was written entitled *Cards Will Destroy Our Country*. The author was aware of the link between playing cards and gambling.

The third thing to be buried was a book of popular songs. Many young people's minds are poisoned by the suggestive words. We congratulate those who made up their minds to avoid such songs and plays, and give praise to God for their decisions.

The fourth was the income of the sake shop and the sake glasses. Many glasses were contributed for burial.

The fifth item consisted of letters from a prostitute, together with her kimono and obi (belt). They were brought by a man who had been saved by faith in Christ.

Also buried was an amulet. Just as a childless woman treasures her dolls, people who have no knowledge of the true God worship wooden, golden and other idols. We who serve the one and only God, the Creator of Heaven and earth, worship him 'in spirit and in truth'.

The six kinds of 'booty' were packed in a box, and one of the sergeants expressed his decision to bury his former pagan faith, together with Satan, declaring that henceforth he would live a Christian life under the leadings of the Holy Spirit.

During the meeting a young Taiwanese man from a school for the blind sang a song, the first verse in Japanese, the second in Taiwanese and the third in English. What an interesting meeting it was! God is alive! Jesus Christ is the Saviour who came to earth to destroy the work of Satan.

Satan buried again
This does not mean that Satan was resurrected, only that we took other satanic items and buried them at a subsequent meeting. When the territorial commander conducted the meeting at Kanda Corps he enrolled four new Salvation Army soldiers. After the enrolment, another 'funeral service' was conducted. The first items to be buried were an amulet from a mountain shrine, and sand and rice from another shrine. It is terrible to worship wooden and golden idols, paper, sand, and so on, while neglecting the true Creator, the blessed God himself. So often idol worship and immorality go hand in hand. Superstition and idols must be destroyed.

The second item was an old cigarette case, together with long pipes which had been broken in two. A convert, over 70 years of age, had stopped smoking and wanted them buried.

The third was a beautiful, expensive pipe. It had been given during the Self-Denial Appeal by a Christian who had determined to stop smoking. He also sold his old books and contributed the money to The Salvation Army.

The fourth included a fine cigarette case, a long pipe, a silver pipe and other articles. They were offered by a young merchant who had repented of their use and had become a Salvation Army soldier.

The fifth item for burial was a cigarette box in which were picture cards given by a boy who attended the children's meeting. Those who like to look at pictures of prostitutes are finally captured by them. This little boy wanted to bury the pictures. God bless him!

The sixth item captured from Satan included a sake bottle and six sake cups. They were offered by a man who had been the victim of sake for 34 years. Now a Salvation Army soldier, he hates sake and gives a strong testimony.

Yes, God is alive! The Salvation Army is an army which overcomes the wiles of Satan through Christ. Everyone who is under the power of Satan should come to The Salvation Army. Glory to God! Praise the name of Jesus Christ!

'Jesus Christ is the same yesterday and today and forever' (Hebrews 13:8). Christ came to earth as a man. He healed the sick, gave life to the dead and did many wonderful works. He is still doing wonderful works in the world, changing bad men into good men, transforming prodigals into persons of integrity, making drunkards into teetotallers, idle men into diligent, liars into honest men, quarrelsome people into people of peace, the worried person into one of trust and serenity. The religion of Jesus Christ is the religion of victory. It is the religion of happiness and peace.

Why not consider this wonderful work of salvation and accept it as God's gift? The founder of Methodism, John Wesley, said on his deathbed, 'The best thing is that God is with us.' This is a truth that all Christian believers experience every day and night.

'Everyone who believes that Jesus is the Christ is born of God, and everyone who loves the father loves his child as well. This is how we know that we love the children of God: by loving God and carrying out his commands. This is love for God: to obey his commands. And his commands are not burdensome, for everyone born of God overcomes the world. This is the victory that has overcome the world, even our faith. Who is it that overcomes the world? Only he who believes that Jesus is the Son of God' (1 John 5:1-5).

Four

The Christian life

I have already spoken about our Heavenly Father in chapter one, about the sins of men in chapter two, and in chapter three about the salvation which sinful man can accept through Christ, in whom we can be reborn. Now I would like to think about how we can keep this salvation and how we can grow and make progress in grace; in short, about the life of the Christian. We should remember, however, that even if we know how but do not put it into practice, our sin before God is very grave. I pray that everyone who reads this chapter has already repented of sin, has exercised faith in Christ, has been forgiven and has experienced his soul's rebirth.

Alexander the Great, when he was young, studied geometry. Finding it difficult, Alexander asked the teacher if there was an easier way to study the subject. 'Like all others,' said the teacher, 'you must follow the highway of learning. There is no byway or shortcut.' Neither is there any shortcut or byway in the realm of religious faith. We have to propel our two legs of repentance and faith, pass through the gate of forgiveness for sin, experience the new birth and worship before the face of our Heavenly Father. 'Salvation is found in no one else, for there is no other name under heaven given to men by which we must be saved' (Acts 4:12). No matter how wide the world or how long the story of history, there is no other Saviour but Christ. And there is no other way of salvation but to return to God in repentance and faith. I pray that God may bless you while you read this book, and that you and all people might be led to this great salvation.

Prayer is important
Prayer is of primary importance in the life of the Christian. There are many greedy, idle men who live bad lives but kneel in front of a Shinto family altar and pray: 'Please keep our family safe; give our business prosperity; send us much money and give us good food; grant us a pleasant life and keep us from punishment when we do wrong.'

Someone wrote: 'If you cannot get an answer to your prayer, it is a sign that your desire is not sincere enough.' However, people can desire with great sincerity the wrong things. Prayer is not like wishing for good luck while one dreams. It is not like waiting under a shelf hoping that a tasty cake will fall from it. Prayer is the heart's sincere desire to talk to God.

It is man's indescribable privilege to pray to the God who is the Creator of all things. We can talk over everything with God. When a man comes to himself, he voluntarily wants to pray. He cannot help praying. In earlier days men who did not know God as a Heavenly Father wrote songs such as, 'I don't know if it's any use praying or not, but there is no one else to rely on but God.' Another said: 'It is God who keeps us, even though we do not pray. It is our need that makes us pray to God.'

The Bible promises that God listens to our prayers. 'Ask and it will be given to you; seek and you will find; knock and the door will be opened to you. For everyone who asks receives; he who seeks finds; and to him who knocks, the door will be opened. Which of you, if his son asks for bread, will give him a stone? Or if he asks for a fish, will give him a snake? If you, then, though you are evil, know how to give good gifts to your children, how much more will your Father in heaven give good gifts to those who ask him! So in everything, do to others what you would have them do to you, for this sums up the Law and the Prophets' (Matthew 7:7-11).

First we have to pray for forgiveness and the rebirth of our soul. When given the blessing of salvation we must pray for strength to overcome all bad habits and to surmount all obstacles in the way of faith. For instance, the converted drunkard who stops drinking might feel that there is nothing further required, but if he is invited by his old friends to drink again, he should at once kneel down and pray: 'O God, though I would like to drink sake, please help me to overcome this temptation.' God will help him, and give him strength to overcome the temptation. Not only sake, but all temptations can be overcome through prayer.

This is the testimony of one Salvationist: 'I used to believe in another god and trusted him to keep me, even when I didn't pray. I disdained praying, and laughed at those who earnestly worshipped God and Buddha and prayed to them. I started to drink sake, and was soon drinking heavily. I began to visit evil places, to my ruination. One day, by chance, I heard of the true God, and had to admit to myself that I was walking the wrong road through life. I repented deeply, and came to realise that there was no one else but Jesus Christ who could cleanse my proud and dirty heart. I had faith in Christ. Now my soul and body are cleansed, and I am enjoying a happy life.'

Praying is not a difficult ceremony. When children speak to their parents there is no formality. The important thing is to pray sincerely and believe that God listens. It is important, too, to pray in the name of Christ. Prayer is like handing a notice of withdrawal to the bank. Christ takes charge and can draw all sorts of blessings out of the exhaustless bank of God. So we should not forget to pray in the name of Jesus Christ: 'Accept our prayers in the name of Christ … I ask these things in the name of Jesus.' Jesus taught the disciples to pray, saying, 'Until now you have not asked for anything in my name. Ask and you will receive, and your joy will be complete' (John 16:24).

David praised God seven times a day. Daniel prayed to God three times a day. Paul taught that we should pray constantly. We should open the door of the day with prayer, and we should close the door of the day with prayer. It is important to pray comprehensively both morning and evening, to pray at the meal table thanking God for food, and to pray for God's help whenever necessary. We should think of God when we walk, do business, read books, or work in the factory. We should seek God's help in everything we do at anytime and anywhere. Not only can we ask for spiritual blessings, we can also ask God to help us physically, in our business, concerning problems about clothing, food and housing. The Bible promises: 'Cast all your anxiety on him because he cares for you' (1 Peter 5:7).

Here is a wonderful example of answered prayer for, truly, God does answer prayer. On 19 June 1891, Juji Ishii, superintendent of the Okayama orphanage, held a prayer in the graveyard behind the orphanage. He asked God to give them some trumpets and an organ. After the prayer meeting he spoke to the orphans and said, 'Seeing we have prayed like this, and as God always answers prayer, he will give us several trumpets, an organ, and two or three more mosquito nets.' One of the orphans scoffingly said, 'Even though you say so, I don't think everything will go as smoothly as you think.'

A few days later someone came to the orphanage and donated some mosquito nets and several trumpets. The instruments were used to summon the children to meals, to meetings and to their studies. The next year, 1892, Mr Ishii was hospitalised for a month. Released, he wrote me a postcard (at the time I was in the college at Kyoto): 'Thank you for all your kindness to me while I was in the hospital in Kyoto. I am getting better. Mr Sharp, who is the teacher at the high school, is offering us an organ. Will you kindly visit him, accept the organ, and send it to us. Regards to my friends Yamamoto, Sasakura, etc.'

I received the postcard on 1 June and asked a friend who could speak English to go with me to see Mr Sharp. The man who came to the door said, 'You say our master is giving away the organ to an orphanage. I can't believe it.' Regardless of the man's surprise, we met Mr Sharp. He led us into a room and showed us the organ, and then asked an old lady to play it. 'What a wonderful organ it is,' Mr Sharp said. 'Will you come and take it away in a few days, when it is convenient?' I made arrangements for the transporting of the organ and then visited Mr Sharp again, together with the mover, who took the organ to Okayama.

God therefore not only answered Ishii's earnest prayer and gave him the trumpets and the mosquito nets, but also provided an organ. It arrived at the orphanage exactly one year from the day of the prayer meeting, 19 June, when Ishii had said, 'This time next year we may have our organ.' Surely it was the work of God, and we could only praise his name.

That night a thanksgiving meeting was held. The boy who a year before had mocked the whole idea was now, like Thomas in the Bible, amazed and praising God, declaring, 'My Lord and my God!' Five years have now passed and I have visited Chugoku, Kyushu and Shikoku. Always I have carried this postcard to remind me that God answers prayer.

People used to say, 'Prayer moves the arm of the One who moves the world.' You can know this for yourself. Earnest prayer is heard by God.

'Do not be anxious about anything, but in everything, by prayer and petition, with thanksgiving, present your requests to God. And the peace of God, which transcends all understanding, will guard your hearts and your minds in Christ Jesus' (Philippians 4:6-7).

Read the Bible

The mother of US President Abraham Lincoln gave him a Bible when he was very young. 'My desire,' she said, 'is not that you should grow tall but that you should read this Bible.' There are two ways in which we can communicate with God. We can speak to God in prayer, and we can read the Bible and discover the will of God for us. Reading the Bible is vitally important in the development of the Christian life.

Just as the body needs three meals a day, so the soul requires to be fed by the Word of God, the Bible. If a Christian fails to read the Bible, his spirit and his faith weaken. He cannot stand the winds and the waves of this world. He becomes like a sickly person who is useless. The Bible explains this truth: 'It is written: "Man does not live on bread alone, but on every word that comes from the mouth of God"' (Matthew 4:4).

The Bible has two parts – the Old Testament and the New Testament. In the Old Testament is recorded the history of God's leadings with men before Christ was born, and the account of the work and the words of those who were faithful to God in ancient times. The New Testament tells of the life of our Saviour, Jesus Christ, and records the works of the disciples, together with their letters. The Scriptures were written by holy men who were inspired by the Holy Spirit. Each portion of the Bible benefits us, especially the New Testament which teaches us about the Saviour, his merciful works, and the ministry of the Holy Spirit. This New Testament should be read first by those who accept God's saving grace.

The Bible relates the wonderful works of God and includes many easily understood parables. There are, too, portions which are strange and difficult to understand. With our finite minds it is impossible to comprehend an infinite God, or to unveil the mystery of life after death. The Bible was written long ago, in distant countries, and in foreign languages which have been translated for us. But we do not read it primarily in order to become a Bible scholar, but rather for the cultivation of our souls and the putting into practice of the will of God. What is plain, we take in. What is difficult to understand, we can skip. Just as a man eats the fish but leaves the bones, so we accept that which we can understand and leave the hard portions until we get to Heaven. Then we will meet and be able freely to converse with the writers.

Dwight L. Moody said that if the rest of the Bible vanished, and only John 3:16 remained, we would still know of God's greatest blessing: 'For God so loved the world that he gave his one and only Son, that whoever believes in him shall not perish but have eternal life' (John 3:16).

Martin Luther was inspired by the one phrase: 'For in the gospel a righteousness from God is revealed, a righteousness that is by faith from first to last, just as it is written: "The righteous will live by faith"' (Romans 1:17). It enabled him to stand for religious reform. Wilberforce, encouraged by the words, 'The battle is not yours, but God's,' devoted himself to the abolition of slavery.

One phrase can get more deeply into a wise man than hundreds of beatings into a foolish man. It is better to read the Bible with sincerity, even if only a small portion, and carry out what it says, than to read long passages daily and fail to put into practice what they say.

It is imperative to make a habit of reading the Bible daily – in the morning, or in the evening. It should be read prayerfully, always seeking for God's help, and always allowing oneself to be guided by the Holy Spirit. Even if we have no other books on our desk, there should be the Bible. All along life's way we should have the companionship of this Book of books.

Oliver Cromwell, a pious man, marched to war singing the Psalms of the Bible. Each of his soldiers was provided with a Bible. One day a soldier returned from battle saying, 'I'm sure I was shot at today, but, strangely, I was not wounded.' The Bible he had taken to war was damaged. The bullet had pierced through the front cover to the centre of the Bible, stopping at Ecclesiastes 12, the first verse of which reads: 'Remember your Creator in the days of your youth.' He was not a religious man but when he saw the marks of the shot and read the verse, his heart was broken. He repented of his sin and began earnestly to serve God.

The famous author Sir Walter Scott, on his deathbed, called his son-in-law and said, 'Bring me a book.'

'What book?' the son-in-law asked.

'There is only one book I need at a time like this – the Bible,' Scott replied. He then asked that the words of Christ recorded in John 14 be read: 'Do not let your hearts be troubled. Trust in God; trust also in me.' Soon after he died peacefully.

When I lived in Kyoto I made friends with a woman who loved to read the Bible. As she was very aged, she found it difficult to remember the order of the books of the Bible, so she made up a song which included the names of the 27 books of the New Testament, and would sing it in order to recall their sequence.

Now I would like to tell you the story of another old lady.

Riseko Morita – a pious woman

The other day a pious woman named Riseko Morita was promoted to Glory. She was a simple countrywoman, but her life was living proof of the grace of God. When she was 25 she married and helped her husband in his business. When she was 47 the husband died, and afterwards she ran a small pawnshop. When she was 61 she left home to travel to several shrines and to visit Kyoto. By mistake she arrived in Osaka, but fortunately had relatives there and stayed with them. All the household were good Christians and Riseko heard from them the story of the true God and, in 1878, received salvation through Christ.

She returned home from Osaka and lived as a Christian. Many of her neighbours were ignorant about Christianity and persecuted her as a magician and a heathen. Even the Shinto and Buddhist priests encouraged the people to annoy Riseko, but she remained steadfast in the faith and prayed earnestly.

Thinking that her faith would be stronger if she could read the Bible, she started to learn the alphabet and eventually began to read the Bible, from which she gained wonderful blessing. In 1886 she built a place for preaching in her neighbourhood, and invited an evangelist to come and proclaim the gospel. In 1892 she built a beautiful chapel in the centre of the village, and the gospel message began to spread.

I went to her home in 1893 and met her. She seemed thrilled to meet me and said, 'It is by the grace of God that you would visit a humble woman like me.' That night we held a special meeting in the chapel. She was busy distributing song books. Watching her during the meeting, I was surprised to see how competent she was in reading the Bible and in singing the hymns. She was now 61, but worked hard from morning to night making handicrafts, studying hard, and raising money for the work of the chapel. She put into practice the biblical instruction, 'Never be lacking in zeal, but keep your spiritual fervour, serving the Lord' (Romans 12:11). Her life was one of fulfilment; she was the first to bring the Christian gospel to the place where she lived. I believe she merited God's 'Well done, thou good and faithful servant.' She was promoted to Glory when 78 years of age.

When we think of a woman who began to learn to read and write after she was 61 years of age because she wanted so earnestly to read the Bible, surely we should read it every day, even a few verses, in order to be blessed of God and taught by him.

'You have known the holy Scriptures, which are able to make you wise for salvation through faith in Christ Jesus. All Scripture is God-breathed and is useful for teaching, rebuking, correcting and training in righteousness, so that the man of God may be thoroughly equipped for every good work' (2 Timothy 3:15-17).

Show your colours
To pray and to read the Bible is necessary. At the same time we must show our colours clearly. But first we must separate ourselves from all worldly activities and cut off any relationships with unclean people. A ship floats on the water, but if the water gets into the ship it sinks. Though we work daily in the world, we must not let the world penetrate our heart, or we will backslide and become a sinner.

In Old Testament times Joseph was courted by the wife of his master, but he refused her and kept himself in purity. Daniel and three other young men refused to eat the king's food, preferring to live simple and clean lives. We must separate ourselves from the evil influences of luxury, frivolity, obscenity, impiety and the harmful customs of this world.

This is most necessary in today's Japan. A Japanese sage once said, 'I looked at the horsefly which flew on to the paper window (*shoji*). I found that it was flying not in the *right* direction, but in the *bright* direction.' Similarly, we Japanese seek after civilisation but, for us, civilisation means trains, steamships, telephones, aeroplanes, factories, enterprises and other things which belong to the surface of civilisation. We forget that the centre of true civilisation is Christianity, and we go round and round in the *bright* direction. As a result we are losing the Samurai spirit of olden times and are failing to take hold of a new faith in God. Politicians are immoral; educators are dissipated; religious men whom many admire cannot regulate their own conduct.

Here is a fool who stole his master's money because he wanted to buy all the prostitutes in Japan. Here is a woman who has been arrested more than 200 times because of prostitution. Everywhere there are quarrels, murders, swindles, adultery. There are 50,000 licensed prostitutes, 60,000 Geisha girls and 60,000 women who serve in the places where men drink sake. All are officially tolerated while they corrupt public morals and harm society. Added to the number are illicit prostitutes and mistresses whose number must be 300,000. The money paid them must be in excess of 300 million yen a year, and what is spent on all this immorality must be more than 7,800 million yen per year. The world is in a depraved situation.

We who belong to Christ do not indulge in such sinful pursuits. But this does not mean we should retire to the mountains and live the life of hermits.

We are in the world but not of it, so we will not be stained by its corrupting influences. We can associate with immoral people in our business, and in our usual association as relatives, friends and neighbours, but always in an effort to lead them into salvation. Apart from this, we should distance ourselves from them.

We should not drink sake, which is the entrance to all sorts of sins. We should not gamble. It is better not to go to plays and films which portray indecency. Many people have become prodigals because they read obscene literature and listened to suggestive stories in variety halls. It is not to our shame if we do not know the taste of *fugu* (a very tasty fish, but one which has poison in part of its body). Rather than being extravagently dressed, we should put on good behaviour. Many items in newspapers and magazines are not worth reading. We should not join in vulgar talk, nor visit immoral places. We should avoid every kind of hurtful worldly activity. The Bible teaches: 'You adulterous people, don't you know that friendship with the world is hatred towards God? Anyone who chooses to be a friend of the world becomes an enemy of God' (James 4:4).

Secondly, we should be willing to be the soldier of God. An ancient scholar declared, 'Give me a place to put the lever, and with it I will move the earth.' If we want to avoid being stained by the world's corruption, and want to help save others from sin, we must find a place to set the lever. For the Christian, it is to join the army of God, confessing our faith in God. This means in The Salvation Army to be enrolled as a soldier, and in the Church to be a member. There is a saying: 'The base of the lighthouse is dark.' But if, instead of one light only, there are two, they help each other, and the whole structure is illumined. The same truth applies to human beings. Even a clever and great man cannot shine everywhere at the same time. On the other hand, if there are two or three ordinary persons, they can help each other escape from falling into sin or failure.

Unity is strength. We need not fight in our own strength alone. When we have the support of God's great army we can fight against the world, against sin and Satan. Jesus said: 'For where two or three come together in my name, there am I with them' (Matthew 18:20). And it is taught in the Letter to the Hebrews, 'Let us not give up meeting together, as some are in the habit of doing, but let us encourage one another – and all the more as you see the Day approaching' (10:25).

I would like to tell you a few stories about showing one's colours clearly. When Madison was president of the USA he had a meal with a group of gentlemen. One raised his glass and, in congratulating the president, invited him to drink. Later, another man encouraged the president to take a drink. Again the president refused. Finally, several of the men urged him to share a toast. The president rose and said, 'Several times I have refused to take a drink. You know my principles. I cannot break the promise I have kept since my youth not to touch liquor. Sixteen friends graduated from the university with me. All of them drank and lived questionable lives. They failed in business, and all have died. Out of the 17 graduates I am now the only one who can work for the good of the people. I have kept my health, happiness and success by the principle of total abstinence. Do you want me to change now, and become your drinking companion?' After the president's speech, there were no further invitations to drink.

A Salvation Army soldier who lives in Okayama testified: 'A few months ago I was invited to the wedding of my cousin's daughter. I knew there would be drinking, so hesitated to attend. But in the end I decided to go. During the celebration there were songs, dances and drinking. They knew I did not drink sake, so they gave me tea and cakes. During the party I took the chance to stand up and say, "I would like you to listen to what I am going to say. I want to offer something from the Word of God to the bride and bridegroom." I then read Ephesians 5:22-33 which speaks of the responsibilities of husband and wife. Both the bride and groom were greatly impressed. We must show our colours clearly. It is honouring to God to confess our faith with boldness, rather than in a cowardly way to keep silent.'

'Do not be yoked together with unbelievers. For what do righteousness and wickedness have in common? Or what fellowship can light have with darkness? What harmony is there between Christ and Belial? What does a believer have in common with an unbeliever? What agreement is there between the temple of God and idols? For we are the temple of the living God. As God has said: "I will live with them and walk among them, and I will be their God, and they will be my people." "Therefore come out from them and be separate, says the Lord. Touch no unclean thing, and I will receive you." "I will be father to you and you will be my sons and daughters, says the Lord Almighty"' (2 Corinthians 6:14-18). 'For it is with your heart that you believe and are justified, and it is with your mouth that you confess and are saved' (Romans 10:10).

Fighting the good fight of faith

Those of us who have severed our relationship with worldly sins and joined the Army of God, and who are clearly showing our colours to the saved and unsaved, should step out and fight the war of faith to save our lost brothers and sisters. Alas, those who have no faith in Christ do not know the value of the soul. They sing: 'You should think of them that serve you. They are the loved and loving children of their parents.' In our heart, we do think of others, and as the song suggests, we think of other people's children as fondly as we think of our own. But this caring does not touch in depth the value of the human soul. The Bible teaches us about this very clearly.

God created man in his own image. God is, therefore, the Father of mankind, and we are his children. The soul of man is more precious than the whole world. God does not want even one soul to perish, so sent his Son, Jesus Christ, to earth to open up the way of salvation. Like a sheep that leaves the fold and strays into the mountains to be torn apart by wolves and lions, man forgets his Heavenly Father and goes astray. He wanders about in a sinful world and at the end becomes the prey of Satan. Christ pitied the lost and came into the world to seek and to save him.

Christ's own parable is recorded in the Bible: 'Suppose one of you has a hundred sheep and loses one of them. Does he not leave the ninety-nine in the open country and go after the lost sheep until he finds it? And when he finds it, he joyfully puts it on his shoulders and goes home. Then he calls his friends and neighbours together and says, "Rejoice with me; I have found my lost sheep." I tell you that in the same way there will be more rejoicing in heaven over one sinner who repents than over ninety-nine righteous persons who do not need to repent' (Luke 15:4-7).

Just like this parable, God regards the soul of man as precious. He cares for each one of us and wants to save us. Through his limitless grace we can be born again. Hallelujah! 'This is love: not that we loved God, but that he loved us and sent his Son as an atoning sacrifice for our sins' (1 John 4:10). 'This is how we know what love is: Jesus Christ laid down his life for us. And we ought to lay down our lives for our brothers' (1 John 3:16). Having had the love of God 'shed abroad in our hearts' we should make every effort to lead those around us into the way of salvation. In this way we can help to repay God's kindness to us.

We have to play our part in life. In our daily work we should strive to make the world better. At the same time we must fight to win the souls of men by leading them to Christ. The Book of Proverbs says, 'Rescue those being led away to death; hold back those staggering towards slaughter. If you say, "But we knew nothing about this," does not he who weighs the heart perceive it? Does not he who guards your life know it? Will he not repay each person according to what he has done?' (24:11, 12).

To save perishing souls is the duty of the saved. To work for the salvation of souls does not always mean standing on a platform and preaching. It can mean visiting the sick and the suffering, inviting others to meetings, praying for others and for the Army, offering money for evangelical work, testifying in meetings to God's blessings, selling *The War Cry*, wearing uniform or the badge of a soldier, joining in marches and working in accordance with the orders and regulations of The Salvation Army.

It should not be thought that this is the work of the officer only. Such precious duties and privileges should be assumed by all Salvation Army soldiers and Christians. The salvation war cannot be fought by a small number of dedicated people only. The revered British Prime Minister Gladstone attended services and read the Bible before the minister preached. The famous politician John Bright was a faithful receptionist at the door of his church. King David sang, 'I would rather be a doorkeeper in the house of my God than dwell in the tents of the wicked' (Psalm 84:10).

The War Cry issued in London, England, contained the following statement: 'There are six million people in London. Imagine each person as a light which has to be lit. If one man has to light them all by himself it will take 11 years, five months and 16 hours to light the six million lights. But if one light lights another, spending one minute for each light, surprisingly, it would take only 24 minutes to light them all. If the number of Salvationists in London is estimated as 10,000, and if each won one convert within a week, only 10 weeks would be necessary to turn London into the Kingdom of God.' Similarly, if all Christians did their part, a mighty revolution, socially and spiritually, would be accomplished.

As the Christian works for the salvation of another, his faith grows. Those who do not work do not grow. It is an obligation to love the souls of men and to work for their salvation.

I spent a summer with one of my friends, Seitaro Yoshida, who was a pious man living in the town of Takahashi in the prefecture of Okayama. He was anxious to lead a strong opponent of the gospel to Christ and visited him often. Always the man said, 'I'm busy, busy, busy.'

'When do you have a free hour?' my friend enquired.

'I have no free hours,' the man replied.

Yoshida pondered the situation and then bought 100 postcards. On each he wrote short sentences about God, Christ, and man's sin, and every day sent several of them to the man. 'Please read any of them when you have a spare moment,' he suggested on the postcards.

Eventually the man said, 'If Yoshida makes such an effort to reach me, then I think I must open my house to him for a meeting.' The gospel message was preached in the man's home and at last he was converted. He became an ardent Christian, and his son a famous social worker.

Mr Yoshida was concerned for those who could not read small printed type, and bought sheets of paper on which he copied the Gospel according to Mark. There is no stronger power than love and no way better than the way of sincerity when stepping out courageously on the soul-winning path.

The following story concerns Miss Phillip, an earnest soldier of The Salvation Army.

An exemplary soldier
Martin Luther, the religious reformer, thanked God for the invention of the printing press as a special manifestation of God's providence. Printing is one of the great weapons which God can use in saving the world. It is a marvellous way of spreading the knowledge of God across the world 'as the waters cover the sea'. Alas, there are those who misuse this divinely-given machine to help the work of Satan, to hurt people and to corrupt their minds. One can see this type of material in newspapers and novels – sensational topics with little root, but big branches and many leaves. If the enemies of God can disturb and harm in this way, then the servants of God should make still greater efforts to triumph in this sphere. That is why The Salvation Army prints a great deal of easily-understood material, to spread the news of salvation throughout the world.

The Salvation Army has various kinds of printed publications. The most widely-known is *The War Cry* which was first issued in London at a halfpenny a copy. Now, in every country where The Salvation Army is working, *The War Cry* is published, in various languages and in varied formats in order to convey the message and mission of the Army. To sell *The War Cry* is a God-given privilege. It is a service to our Heavenly Father. European Salvationists are most earnest in selling copies of *The War Cry*. Many sell 200 or 300 copies per week.

I would like to tell you what kind of effort Salvationists in other countries make to distribute copies. Miss Phillip is an English girl working as a servant. Though only a servant girl she is a courageous worker for Christ, always seeking the salvation of others. As she has much to do in the house, she has only one night a week free. On that free night she visits the public houses with copies of *The War Cry*, speaking to prodigals and drunkards. She sings Army songs to them, prays with them and testifies to the salvation she has found in Christ. She urges her hearers to repent. She sells 50 to 70 copies of *The War Cry* during the hours of her one free evening, which she gives to God.

In England, the first step towards a life of sin is often taken in the public houses where there is strong drink, evil companions and dirty talk, all of which lead to degeneration. As Miss Phillip wants to make the most of her one free evening a week, she goes into these dens of evil by herself in an effort to win men back to God. The publican does not like her. Drunkards persecute her. But she rejoices in the opposition and keeps on boldly and cheerfully with her work. General William Booth said, 'Go for souls and go for the worst.' That is the mission of the Army. Miss Phillip works in that spirit, and is a fine example of the Blood and Fire soldier.

Her testimonies are always alive with interesting incidents. She once saw a young woman soliciting a man on a street corner. Miss Phillip remonstrated with the girl, who immediately sought salvation. A man, after hearing Miss Phillip speak in a public house came to the Salvation Army hall and found salvation. One night, in a public house, she began to sing, 'I Heard the Voice of Jesus Calling'. As she sang, the drunkards stopped talking. As she continued, glasses were put on the tables. Everyone sensed the presence of God's Spirit. The innkeeper, however, was annoyed and shouted: 'Call the police. I want this woman out of my premises.' But no one moved. Some of the customers were moved to repentance and God was glorified by their surrender to him. At the end, even the publican was moved, and said to Miss Phillip, 'Please come again.'

Recently, in one evening she sold 78 copies of *The War Cry*. One publican refused her admittance into his tavern, but she smiled and pushed past him and began to sing, 'Jesus is Praying for Me in Heaven'. A young man spoke out and said, 'That is the song my mother sang when I was very young. Now she is in Heaven, and here I am wandering around the public houses.' He began to weep.

Miss Phillip is not only a good saleswoman, but a powerful evangelist – a servant girl who is making every possible effort to win souls for Christ. Concerned about the poor children of her neighbourhood, Miss Phillip canvassed nearby homes and collected enough money for the corps to give a special meal to 180 needy youngsters. Concerned about the famine-stricken people of

India, she asked for special donations. A man challenged her saying, 'You are not collecting money for the people of India, but for yourself.' Finally she had to go to the police station with the drunken man to settle the matter. The police, however, knew the Salvationist and added their donations. The drunkard felt ashamed of what he had said and done, and left the police station after making his own contribution.

A Salvation Army major visiting Miss Phillip asked her the secret of her victories. Her reply was, 'I do what I am told to do by God, whenever he speaks, and no matter where I am.' It is a fact that her cheerfulness, courage, singing and preaching help her greatly, but the most important thing is that she leaves everything to God and acts according to his guidance. This is the real secret of her success.

The Salvation Army exists not only by the power of General Booth and its organisation and principles, but also by the courageous fight of faith, in a Blood and Fire spirit, of those who make up its ranks – servants, servant-girls, apprentices in shops and factories, grooms, labourers, and so on. The Army relies on the work done by people like Miss Phillip. Stand up, soldiers of the Army! Most of you have more free time, more talents, more influence than Miss Phillip. Why can you not accomplish as great a work as her, and an even greater work?

'Jesus replied: "A certain man was preparing a great banquet and invited many guests. At the time of the banquet he sent his servant to tell those who had been invited, 'Come, for everything is now ready.' But they all alike began to make excuses. The first said, 'I have just bought a field, and I must go and see it. Please excuse me.' Another said, 'I have just bought five yoke of oxen, and I'm on my way to try them out. Please excuse me.' Still another said 'I have just got married, so I can't come.' The servant came back and reported this to his master. Then the owner of the house became angry and ordered his servant, 'Go out quickly into the streets and alleys of the town and bring in the poor, the crippled, the blind and the lame.' 'Sir,' the servant said, 'what you ordered has been done, but there is still room.' Then the master told his servant, 'Go out to the roads and country lanes and make them come in, so that my house will be full. I tell you, not one of those men who were invited will get a taste of my banquet'" (Luke 14:16-24).

Receive the Holy Spirit

There is one other thing which is most important, in the life of the Christian, and that is to receive the Holy Spirit. Firstly, the Holy Spirit cleanses the heart. John the Baptist was born six months before Christ. He was clothed with camel's hair, wore a girdle of skin about his loins and ate locusts and wild honey. He gathered many people together, reproached them for their sinfulness, and urged them to repent. When they did, he led them into the water as a sign of true repentance, and then prayed with them, telling them he could only baptise them with water, but Jesus would baptise them with the Holy Spirit, who would burn out all their impurity.

Jesus spent three years working among the people and finally died on the cross as an atonement for the sin of mankind. He then gave the Holy Spirit to regenerate and to empower. As fire burns out impurities, so the Holy Spirit cleanses the heart. Those so cleansed can live a life without sin in the power of the Spirit.

Jesus said whoever looks lustfully at a woman has already committed adultery with her in his heart (see Matthew 5:28). Only by the indwelling of the Spirit can men avoid such condemnation. The Bible says Enoch walked with God for 300 years and lived according to God's will. William Booth described Enoch as 'the first Salvationist'.

Secondly, the Holy Spirit teaches and guides us. The Spirit of God is a wonderful teacher. When George Fox was 19 years of age he took a walk with a cousin and one of his friends. They went to a restaurant and the friend said, 'Let's have a drink. The one who doesn't drink pays for all.' George was perplexed. He couldn't understand why his cousin and his friend, who confessed themselves to be Christians, and who knew it was wrong to drink, should encourage others to do so. He then said, 'I'll pay the bill' and, leaving the money on the table, went home and began to pray, asking God to reveal his will. The Holy Spirit reminded him that, 'Young people seek after vanity and elderly people seek after the things of this world. You should be separated from them and become a gentile, completely.' From then on he followed totally the leadings of the Holy Spirit, and later became the founder of the Society of Friends.

George Müller, as I have already mentioned, looked after thousands of children. Every day he prayed earnestly for the Holy Spirit's guidance in everything he did, even for guidance in searching for a lost door-key. So must we seek the Spirit's guidance in everything we do.

One of our Army soldiers in Tokyo told me a moving story. She was an old woman who sold salt at her house. 'I was told,' she said, 'by the owner of my house to leave. Not only me, but all who lived in the place were told to move out. All except me found another place to live. People would not rent me a house because I was a Christian. I was then given one day's notice to leave, but had nowhere to go. I knelt down and prayed, "Please, God, find a house for me." That evening I did not eat, but kept on praying.

'While I was praying a ragman came and said, "There is an empty house in front of the Salvation Army hall." I thought this must be the providence of God, but on reaching the place found it was not empty after all. The man of the house had put a number of articles on a cart and was going to sell them. Mistakenly, the ragman had thought the man was moving elsewhere. I was really disappointed, but began to think that God must have led me to this place and must have had something in mind for me. I went down the street, passing the Salvation Army home for ex-prisoners, and found an empty house. But it had no roof. It had been carried away in a windstorm. How could anyone live in a house without a roof? I stood on the spot and prayed again.

'While I was doing so, a friend came up to me and said, "What are you doing?" I said, "I'm praying to God to give me a house." He laughed and said, "What nonsense are you talking? If you want an empty house, look over there." I went to the place he pointed out and found an empty house which I could rent. The next morning I moved in. Now I don't hear the threats of my old landlord, and my new home is so much nearer the Salvation Army that I can attend all the meetings. I thank God for his grace.'

Someone has said, 'We should not hesitate to bring our cares to God. We can leave them with him.' We must seek the Holy Spirit's guidance in everything.

Thirdly, the Holy Spirit gives power. The Bible says, 'God chose the foolish things of the world to shame the wise; God chose the weak things of the world to shame the strong. He chose the lowly things of this world and the despised things – and the things that are not – to nullify the things that are' (1 Corinthians 1:27, 28). God often chooses illiterate people, gives them the power of the Holy Spirit, and allows them to do wonderful works. Few of Christ's disciples were educated men. Most were fishermen, a tax-collector and men of ordinary occupations. But by the Spirit they did mighty works. The Acts of the Apostles is the Acts of the Holy Spirit through the Apostles.

John Bunyan was uneducated. Led by the Spirit he wrote *The Pilgrim's Progress*, which has been read by more people throughout the world than any book written by scholars and famous authors in the past 200 years.

One day a person greeted Commissioner Elijah Cadman, as he thought for the first time. The commissioner, however, said, 'I have been to your house before.'

'When was that?' the man asked, 'I have no memory of it.'

The commissioner smiled and said, 'I went to your home to clean the chimney before I became an officer of The Salvation Army.'

Let us praise the God who can raise a chimney sweep to be a successful worker in The Salvation Army and lead many people to Christ.

God not only uses illiterate and ordinary people to work out his will but also cleanses and calls men of talent and education. The Apostle Paul is a splendid example. In short, God can use men with great powers and he can use men who have few powers. Whoever opens his heart and invites the Spirit of God into its most innermost room can be filled with the Spirit of God and be sustained by divine grace. Woe to those who invite the Holy Spirit into their heart but who give precedence to such visitors as improper sexual desires and other sins, and to those who rent the room of their heart to evil and refuse to accept the Holy Spirit. The heart must first be emptied of sin, then we can pray for an infilling of the Spirit. Such an infilling will come to those who sincerely pray for it and seek after it.

'On one occasion, while he was eating with them, he gave them this command: "Do not leave Jerusalem, but wait for the gift my Father promised, which you have heard me speak about. For John baptised with water, but in a few days you will be baptised with the Holy Spirit." So when they met together, they asked him, "Lord, are you at this time going to restore the kingdom to Israel?" He said to them: "It is not for you to know the times or dates the Father has set by his own authority. But you will receive power when the Holy Spirit comes on you; and you will be my witnesses in Jerusalem, and in all Judea and Samaria, and to the ends of the earth"' (Acts 1:4-8). 'If you then, though you are evil, know how to give good gifts to your children, how much more will your Father in Heaven give the Holy Spirit to those who ask him!' (Luke 11:13).

Five

The Christian's responsibility

Our life in this world is like the movement of the watermill. If the watermill's wheel is completely under water it is of no use; and if it is entirely out of the water it will not turn. A man who uses deception to win the favour of others and gain material wealth is like a watermill under water. He will float down the river of worldliness. And if a man disdains this world, viewing it as transient and full of cares, and simply goes up into the mountain to live as a hermit, he is like a watermill high out of the water. He cannot do anything worthwhile. But put part of the watermill's wheel into the water and it moves according to the flow of the stream. Its upper part is out of the water, and moves in the opposite direction to the flow of the stream. Positioned properly, the watermill fulfils its role.

The life of the Christian soldier is like a working watermill. He or she lives in the world, dwells among the people, does his or her daily work together with others. But such soldiers' hearts look up to God as they stand against the sins of this world and live holy lives. The Christian soldier lives in this world but does not belong to it, doesn't flee from the sins of this world and take refuge in a mountain cave. Instead, he or she fights to destroy the sins of this world.

That is what Jesus meant when he prayed for his disciples: 'My prayer is not that you take them out of the world but that you protect them from the evil one' (John 17:15).

Now I would like to think about how we who are saved and belong to the Army of God should live in this world.

You are the salt of the earth

Jesus said to the believers, 'You are the salt of the earth' (Matthew 5:13). This is a short sentence but it teaches many lessons. Firstly, the most essential thing about salt is not that it is white, or fine, but that it is salty. Our figure, our face, or the amount of our income or our standard of living matter little. What counts is the 'saltiness' of our faith and spirit. King Saul had an impressive figure. He was 'without equal among the Israelites – a head taller than any of the others' (1 Samuel 9:2). But he stood against God and acted selfishly, and was punished. A young David, only 22 or 23 years of age, succeeded him on the throne. In choosing David as King, God said: 'Do not consider his appearance or his height . . . The LORD does not look at the things man looks at. Man looks at the outward appearance, but the LORD looks at the heart' (1 Samuel 16:7).

We must preserve the salty taste of Christian principle and integrity, and not allow ourselves to be robbed of it.

Secondly, if we put salt in a bottle or bag and simply store it, it has no usefulness. Salt is useful only if it is used; when, for example, it is put into food when cooking. Likewise, the soldier of Christ, following his own occupation or profession, goes out into the world, upholding Christian standards. He does not leave the world, nor is he left by the world. He is not a recluse, of no use to this world.

Thirdly, the effect of salt is to cleanse, to stop corruption, to give flavour to food. Similarly, Christians go into the world to purify society, to stop the corruption of public morals, to do the will of God and to glorify him.

George Fox was a shoemaker. He was a man who always kept his promises, worked hard and kept his own counsel. He was trusted by everyone. All who knew him relied on his word. Once he had used the word, 'truly', what he said or did was always true.

William Ewart Gladstone had a noble spirit, and while a university student influenced his friends to become Christians.

In a country town on the Island of Shikoku there was a smithy who was one of the pillars of the local church. While he hammered the molten iron day after day he spoke about the gospel to all who came into his foundry. Like him, we should hammer our Christian principles into our daily work. A kimono dyer was once asked, 'How can you make such beautiful colours?'

'I mix my mind with the colours,' he answered. We should pour our faith into our tasks, and so accomplish work that cannot be imitated by the people of the world.

Needless to say, we should do this not only in our business but in all our dealings with people and in every circumstance. An educated preacher wanted to lead his neighbour, a lawyer, into the Christian faith. Fortunately, the lawyer attended the services every Sunday, and the minister often shaped his sermons to appeal to the solicitor's sense of logic. One day the lawyer said he had decided to become a Christian. The preacher was greatly pleased and said, 'I'm glad to hear it. Perhaps I could make a guess as to which of my sermons persuaded you to follow the Christian faith?'

'I wasn't persuaded by any of your sermons,' the lawyer answered. 'I've been thinking about the Christian faith for many years. But last Sunday, as I left the church, old Anna was going down the stone steps. I went to her and helped her. She was so grateful, and looking at me said, "Do you love my Saviour Jesus, too?" Her earnest voice sounded like the voice of Jesus himself to me. I thought and thought, and gradually the doubts of many years disappeared, and now I confess my faith in Christ.'

The words and acts of sincere Christians often speak more, and affect others more, than the sermons of great preachers. A man sat in a tea-house near the temple and ate his rice cakes. While resting he sat looking at the lake. Several students come into the tea-house. They ate several dishes of rice cake, put their hands into their pockets and took out some money which they put on the table before leaving. The manager came to the table, scooped up the money but did not count it.

The man looked at the manager and asked, 'What if there is a mistake in the amount of money the students left, seeing you didn't count it?' The manager's wife answered, 'There will be no mistake. They are students of the Christian university in Kyoto.'

That Christianity had such power to influence people greatly impressed the customer. Returning home, he visited a Christian evangelist in his neighbourhood and inquired about the faith. As a result, the man repented of his sins and became an earnest Christian. The Bible tells us, 'So whether you eat or drink or whatever you do, do it all for the glory of God' (1 Corinthians 10:31).

When God decided to destroy the two sinful cities of Sodom and Gomorrah, he said he wanted to forgive both cities, providing he could find 10 righteous men in Sodom. But as he could not find 10 he would have to destroy it. We, the soldiers of Christ, should be the 10 righteous. If worldly people serve sin and Satan, we should stand firm on Christian principles and against sin in order to protect the world from corruption, and to reflect God's will in our daily work. We should be 'the salt of the earth', influencing others for good.

'You are the salt of the earth. But if the salt loses its saltiness, how can it be made salty again? It is no longer good for anything, except to be thrown out and trampled by men. You are the light of the world. A city on a hill cannot be hidden. Neither do people light a lamp and put it under a bowl. Instead they put it on its stand, and it gives light to everyone in the house. In the same way, let your light shine before men, that they may see your good deeds and praise your Father in Heaven' (Matthew 5:13-16).

Seek first the Kingdom of God

Just as a person's body has eyes, nose, ears, mouth, hands and feet, so there is a variety of occupations for man – merchants, farmers, sailors, scholars, government officials and so on. God created men and women with different gifts and capacities and gave to each the kind of employment that would enable them to make a particular contribution to the betterment of society. There are the rich and the poor in this world. God made them all. One will pull a cart; another will ride in it. One will rule the people; others will be ruled. One will employ people; others will be employed by him or her. One will cultivate the rice plant; others will eat the rice. We should not think of the one who rides in the cart as important, and the one who pulls it as lowly.

We should not think of the one who tends the rice paddy as superior to the one who eats the rice. Whether the man is lowly or not depends not on his occupation but on his attitude to that occupation.

Admiral Lord Nelson said, 'I will be as faithful to my work if only entrusted with one small barge as if I were in command of the entire British Navy.' There is a Japanese story of a servant who said to his master, 'You, who are paid a great salary, have one life only. I, who have only a small salary, have only one life. We both have the some precious life. I would like to demonstrate that equality by carrying your shoes or your luggage.'

We should not feel ashamed of our occupation. It does not matter what kind of work we do. We should be grateful to God for his many blessings and should do our tasks earnestly and faithfully – in fact, more faithfully than any other. As carpenters, plasterers, smithies, servants, merchants, we should work devotedly to glorify God and to fulfil his will for us in this world.

Labour need not be the curse of sin for us. It can be a gift of God's grace. It need not be a heavy burden, but rather a joy. Labour can be a prayer of praise and thanksgiving to God. Throughout the ages, pious people have worked untiringly and well. In the Bible are the biographies of those who considered their labour to be sacred. Abraham, who was called 'the father of the faith', kept many oxen and sheep. His descendants, Isaac and Jacob, were similarly employed. Joseph, who looked after the house of his lord, became an outstanding and tactful prime minister. Moses, Amos, David and other notable personalities were labourers of one kind or another. Our Saviour, Jesus Christ, worked as a carpenter, and chose his disciples from the labouring class. Paul, the apostle to the Gentiles, supported himself in his evangelical work by making tents. He warned idle believers by saying, 'If any would not work, neither should he eat.'

Those who live by God's Word and work diligently will have peace in their heart. Even if one is poor, he or she can have the kind of happy life which others cannot even imagine.

Mr Amamiya was thrown into jail for bribery. He was allowed 15 minutes a day for physical exercise, but wanted more. Flattering the jailer, he said, 'I hear you work very hard every day but are paid only a small salary. When I'm released I'll make every effort to see that you are better treated.'

The jailer asked, 'How much money do you have?'

'At home, a great deal,' the prisoner replied.

The jailer laughed and said, 'You may have lots of money, but you have to stay in jail. I may not have much money, but I'm happier than you are. I can enjoy freedom.'

The Book of Proverbs says: 'Better a little with the fear of the Lord than great wealth with turmoil.

Better a meal of vegetables where there is love than a fattened calf with hatred' (15:16-17).

True peace and happiness will not remain in the heart unless the presence of Christ is there. Peace and happiness dwell in the hearts of those who do their duty faithfully before God even if they are without material possessions. Christ did not have a place to lay his head through all the years of his ministry. He wandered through the countryside and experienced hunger and fatigue. But he could say, 'Blessed are the poor in spirit' (Matthew 5:3), 'Blessed are the meek' (Matthew 5:5), 'Blessed are the pure in heart (Matthew 5:8), 'Blessed are those who are persecuted because of righteousness' (Matthew 5:10). Christ was himself a witness to the fact that poor people can have a happy life, despite their poverty.

Moreover, those who do work well and follow God's leadings can become wealthy. A man who sold charcoal in downtown Tokyo had a friend who bought empty casks for resale. 'You buy empty casks,' he said, 'and I sell charcoal. We both work hard and our work is a service to earth and Heaven.'

Whatever the occupation – buying empty casks, selling charcoal, serving as a soldier or banking – each should do his best in his work. To acquire money should not be the only incentive. Why seek money simply to hide in the house? Work hard. Do not think of yourself as poor. If Heaven and earth are served by your toil, money will come naturally, and God will give you happy days. The Christian will not be greedy, always wanting more money than he deserves. The charcoal seller said his work was 'to serve Heaven and earth'. This means doing one's best in the occupation given by God.

It is said: 'Reason is interest; virtue is profit. If one gets a new heart, he will get new clothes.' To those who seek after God's Kingdom and his righteousness, God gives clothing, food, shelter and all else that is necessary. And this is true not only spiritually, but materially as well.

'No one can serve two masters. Either he will hate the one and love the other, or he will be devoted to the one and despise the other. You cannot serve both God and Money. Therefore I tell you, do not worry about your life, what you will eat or drink; or about your body, what you will wear. Is not life more important than food, and the body more important than clothes? Look at the birds of the air; they do not sow or reap or store away in barns, and yet your heavenly Father feeds them. Are you not much more valuable than they? Who of you by worrying can add a single hour to his life? And why do you worry about clothes? See how the lilies of the field grow. They do not labour or spin. Yet I tell you that not even Solomon in all his splendour was dressed like one of these. If that is how God clothes the grass of the field, which is here today and tomorrow is thrown into the fire, will he not much more clothe you, O you of little faith? So do not worry, saying, "What shall we eat?" or "What shall we drink?" or "What shall we wear?" For the pagans run after all these things, and your heavenly Father knows that you need them. But seek first his Kingdom and his righteousness, and all these things will be given to you as well. Therefore do not worry about tomorrow, for tomorrow will worry about itself. Each day has enough trouble of its own' (Matthew 6:24-34).

Salvation means good health
Many religions emphasise the fact that if people have a strong faith they can recover from illness and have good health. Some say prayer is the antidote to an epidemic of sickness. Others provide holy water to wash away illness. Still others observe special ceremonies to fend off the causes of illness. There are those who distribute candies impregnated with strange medicines. So many ways, people say, to expel sickness through religious exercises. Well, how about our Christian faith?

We do not deceive people when inviting them to become Christians. We do not bait them with the prospect of healing or of acquiring wealth. We emphasise the all-important necessity for repentance from sin and faith in Christ, the forgiveness of sins, the blessing of the new birth of the soul, and the possibility of living a happy life which is completely different to a past, sinful life.

These are our foundations. We cannot gain faith in God by any other ways. As Paul said: 'For physical training is of some value, but godliness has value for all things, holding promise for both the present life and the life to come' (1 Timothy 4:8).

God looks after our soul, and he looks after our physical needs as well. On earth, Christ gave salvation to the miserable sinner. He also healed the sick and aided the disabled. We, therefore, who have been forgiven of our sins and who now live happy and pure lives, can receive the blessing of God on our physical body. Jesus Christ is the friend of the sick, the weak and the aged who are infirm. Hallelujah! The sparrow does not fall to the earth without his knowledge, and even the hairs of our head are numbered by him. This makes for peace in the heart of the Christian.

People of this world fall ill sometimes because of intemperance. Soldiers of Christ, however, can deny themselves and rise above the desires of the flesh. Dissipation plagues the body, but the Christian does not indulge in those things that lead to degeneration

The smallest sparrow cannot be caught by man if God does not permit it. How graciously the Heavenly Father cares for every one of us! The soldier of Christ lives without fear because God is with him, even if a thousand fall in front of him and 10,000 behind him.

The soldier of Christ commits everything to God. That is why Christian patients are an encouragement and blessing to those who visit them in hospital or in their homes. Those who know how to live, know how to die. They accept God's will, they enjoy God's leadings in their lives, they bear sufferings which others find impossible to carry. This is one of the blessings true believers experience. As ours is a living Lord we entrust all to him. He accepts our all, and deals with us in perfect ways. Many who have served God loyally have been granted recovery from serious illness, thus enabling them to go on serving God in good health.

Doctors treating Cardinal Newman's raging fever feared for his life. His comment was, 'I have a God-given duty to serve England. I will not die until that task is finished.' He recovered and pursued his effective ministry. William Booth, Founder of The Salvation Army, was not a strong youth. When 17 or 18 years of age he aspired to be an evangelist, but the doctor said that if he took up such exhausting work he would die within a year. He lived to be 83 years of age, and accomplished more than six or seven ordinary men would have done. While in Australia he came down with typhoid fever but recovered within a week. Such a recovery could hardly be the work of man, but of God. Christ, who saves our soul, can heal the body. 'And the prayer offered in faith will make the sick person well; the Lord will raise him up. If he has sinned, he will be forgiven' (James 5:15). This is God's promise recorded in the Bible.

'Is any one of you in trouble? He should pray. Is anyone happy? Let him sing songs of praise. Is any one of you sick? He should call the elders of the church to pray over him and anoint him with oil in the name of the Lord. And the prayer offered in faith will make the sick person well; the Lord will raise him up. If he has sinned, he will be forgiven. Therefore confess your sins to each other and pray for each other so that you may be healed. The prayer of a righteous man is powerful and effective' (James 5:13-16).

Love begins at home

When Christ saw that Zacchaeus sincerely repented, he said, 'Today salvation has come to this house' (Luke 19:9). When Paul and Silas saw the fear of their jailer they exhorted him to 'believe in the Lord Jesus, and you will be saved – you and your household' (Acts 16:31). Salvation through Christ should be brought into the home.

Strictly speaking, there are few homes in Japan today that deserve to be called 'home'. There are only houses, or residences for people. I was surprised when I looked at a copy of one man's family register. He was highly respected, a head priest, and many wanted to drink even the water from his bath. Yet he had many mistresses and illegitimate children. Even so-called religious men have that sort of family, and it is little wonder that ordinary men have mistresses and prostitutes, and that there is in the house adultery, divorce, quarrelling, drinking, jealousy, anger, sadness, woe, obscene literature, arguments over family estates, fisticuffs and even murders. How can men and women who live in sin and depravity have good homes?

The other day I read the diaries of schoolgirls written while on holiday. They were shown to me by one of the teachers. Reading them I again felt the need for the homes of Japan to be saved through the Blood of Christ. Allow me to quote from the diaries:

'1st day: I got up and went to buy flowers. After I came back Mother gave me money and I went to buy sweets. I had lunch, and Mother hit me on my back. I was very angry. I had a nap, got up, and washed my face. I went to meet some friends without telling my Mother. When I was called I came home and slept at the entrance. I quarrelled with my brother while we were eating breakfast. I had to take my younger sister to the toilet. I complained about it, and handled her roughly. I fought my two sisters. We used strong language. I called my Mother a foolish old woman and said nasty words against my parents.'

This girl was only 14 years of age. Her father worked as a masseur, and her mother worked at home making cigarettes. The parents wanted the girl to get work so they could have some cash.

'21st. I got up late in the morning and quarrelled with my grandmother. I was angry all day and went to bed early.

'22nd. I read novels all day.

'23rd. I got up early and complained that I had no coat, so I put on a kimono and was scolded by my mother. I did some knitting in the afternoon and went out in the evening. I come home late.

'25th. I got up late and played by myself at home. In the afternoon my friend come to the front of the house and called me, but I did not reply. Father scolded me. I went out to the night stalls, came back and went to bed.

'26th. I got up early and swept the garden, went shopping and did some knitting. In the afternoon I went out to the stalls and came back late in the evening.

'27th. In the morning I went on an errand. After that I played by myself at home. In the evening went to the variety hall.

'28th. I got up early, swept the garden, read a textbook, went to the stalls in the afternoon and went to the variety hall in the evening.

'3rd. Helped with the housework, cleaning the rooms. Went to the variety hall in the evening.'

This girl is 12 years of age. Her father is a government official and her mother works as a hairdresser. She read novels, visited the night stalls and the variety hall. She quarrelled with her grandmother and was angry all day. What will be the future for this kind of girl?

Jesus said, 'The axe is already at the root of the trees, and every tree that does not produce good fruit will be cut down and thrown into the fire'

(Matthew 3:10). I am afraid that such corrupt families will bear evil fruit in the future.

I read many diaries like these, and found only one that gave me hope and joy. Here it is.

'25th. I got up at three o'clock in the morning and went to the kitchen and pumped water out of the well as silently as possible, and then cleaned the garden. It was four o'clock when I finished. I opened the gate and saw a tramp sleeping. I woke him up and said, "Go quickly. Anyone seeing you here would tell you off." He said he was hungry and could not stand up. I went into the house and got some food for him. He was so pleased and went away. When I returned to the house my Mother was making a fire. I told my parents and brothers about the tramp. They were pleased to hear what I had done.

'26th. I looked after my elder brother who was sick in bed. He become sick on the 25th, and appreciated my looking after him. At his bedside I read a book to him. He was pleased. My brother became more seriously ill.

'30th. My brother's friends came to see him. I went to Tokyo hospital to see my eldest sister. She was greatly pleased. I spent half a day with her. She gave me medicine for my brother. When I came home I told my parents about the medicine and gave it to my brother. He was so grateful that he shed tears. In the evening I read a book and then went to bed.

'1st. It was Sunday. I got up at seven. My elder brother got well, and I went to church with him. When I come home the maid handed me a letter. It said that a friend of mine had been seriously hurt. I went to her house. She was bandaged and in bed. She said she had fallen down the cliff at the back of their house. I sat near her and cried. We had been very good friends since we were small. I like her very much. I thought she looked very miserable and I could not stop crying. I spoke words of comfort to her. As it was dark I had to come home, but she did not want me to leave. I didn't want to go, either, but I said goodbye and left. I cried in my bed . . . My brother asked me to go on an errand. It was raining, and on my way home I saw an old woman under a tree. She was sheltering there because she did not have an umbrella. I went up to her and asked where her house was. It was several blocks beyond our home but I took her to her house. Her daughter thanked me. When I got home my brother said, "You're very late." I explained why, and my parents said I had done a good deed. I was pleased.

'8th. It was Sunday. I went to church in the morning. I testified in the meeting, and the congregation was pleased to hear my words. In the evening I went to church once again. On my way home I was alone and it was dark. I had to walk along a bank. I reached home and went to bed at ten o'clock.'

Compare this last diary with the previous two. The difference is marked, like the difference between Heaven and earth. This girl's family was richer than other families, but the relationship between the parents and the child, between brothers and sisters and friends, was warm and pure, and they loved each other. This is the result of the Christian faith of the family. They rely upon the Spirit's leadings in all that they do.

The reformer Martin Luther was greatly troubled at one period and agonised alone in his room. His wife wanted to comfort him, so she dressed herself in the black clothes worn only at funerals. Entering her husband's room she stood beside him. He asked, 'Who has died? Whose funeral are you going, to?'

She answered, 'God has died.'

'Don't say such foolish things, said Martin Luther, 'God is alive. He does not die.'

'If that is so,' said his wife, 'why are you, who trust in him, so sad and discouraged?'

For 16 years a woman named Monica made efforts to bring her husband back to God. For 30 years she tried to bring her son, Augustine, back to the ways of righteousness. She succeeded on both counts. Later, out of gratitude, Augustine said, 'I drank in the name of Jesus with my mother's milk.'

There is no quarrelling in the home of true Christians. One wife cares for one husband. One husband cares for one wife. Children love their parents, and parents nurture their children as gifts from God. This is what the Bible says: 'Wives, submit to your husbands, as is fitting in the Lord. Husbands, love your wives and do not be harsh with them. Children, obey your parents in everything, for this pleases the Lord. Fathers, do not embitter your children, or they will become discouraged. Slaves, obey your earthly masters in everything; and do it, not only when their eye is on you and to win their favour, but with sincerity of heart and reverence for the Lord. Whatever you do, work at it with all your heart, as working for the Lord, not for men, since you know that you will receive an inheritance from the Lord as a reward. It is the Lord Christ you are serving. Anyone who does wrong will be repaid for his wrong, and there is no favouritism' (Colossians 3:18-25).

'Masters, provide your slaves with what is right and fair, because you know that you also have a Master in Heaven' (Colossians 4:1).

In the home of the true soldier of Jesus Christ everyone puts into practice this wonderful teaching. All in the home revere the God who sees all, despite every effort of man to hide things from him. Christ is the head of the house. Everything that is done in the home is in accordance with God's will. Every Christian should take the message of salvation into the home.

How can this be done? The first member of the family to be saved should invite the other members of the family to the meetings, and should encourage them to read the Bible. If possible, a cottage meeting should be held daily, or a few times each week, so that members of the family may be led to know Christ. It is said that 'love begins at home'. We should make every effort to share with our families the blessings God has given us.

'Now fear the LORD and serve him with all faithfulness. Throw away the gods your forefathers worshipped beyond the River and in Egypt, and serve the LORD. But if serving the LORD seems undesirable to you, then choose for yourselves this day whom you will serve, whether the gods your forefathers served beyond the River, or the gods of the Amorites, in whose land you are living. But as for me and my household, we will serve the LORD' (Joshua 24:14-15).

To die is gain

A feudal lord had a jester who would perform for him in his times of depression. He often called on the fool and enjoyed his performances. One day he gave his jester a stick and said, 'Keep this stick carefully and when you find a person who is more foolish than yourself, pass over the stick.' The jester accepted the stick and took it with him everywhere. Even when he slept, the stick was beside his bed. Always he was looking for a person more foolish than himself to whom he could present the stick.

One day the master took ill and his sickness increased in seriousness. People said that the lord's life would soon end. The lord summoned the jester to him once again and said, 'You have been with me for many years, but now I have to say goodbye to you. I am going on a long journey.'

The jester was surprised and enquired as to what preparations his master had made for such a long journey.

'I have not made any preparations,' said the lord, 'and I will start on my journey when I close my eyes.'

The jester asked, 'When will you return?'

'The place I am going to is far away,' said the lord, 'and no one has ever returned from it.'

The jester thought for a while and then took the stick and said, 'My lord, now I will give this stick to you.'

The jester knew that even for a short journey people take money and food with them, but the lord had said he was leaving on a very long journey and had made no preparations. The jester thought his lord was far more foolish than himself.

According to sociologists, 22 million people die every year in the world. That is 3,674 persons every hour, or 62 every minute. This means at least one person dies every second. We do not know when it will be our turn. Man's life is transient. 'One does not possess tomorrow; the cherry blossoms can be blown away in one night of storm.' We should make our preparations for death while we are in good health, and be ready to die, without fear, at any time.

Some people deceive themselves by thinking that if they have a prosperous life, with plenty of money in this world, it doesn't matter whether they die or not, or where they may go after death. The Bible, however, teaches that a man's life does not consist of his possessions.

Money, honour and fame cannot remove man's fear of death. One of England's queens, on her deathbed, said to the servants around her, 'If any of you can extend my life, I will grant whatever you want.' None could meet her request, and the queen died in sadness.

Hideyoshi Toyotomi came out of a small country town, and later become a regent and ruled Korea. He built a big castle and gained fame and honours. But when dying he wrote a farewell poem: 'My life was like the dew; it came like dew, and disappeared like dew. Everything is just a dream.'

An old woman in Hiroshima who had no children or other relatives had saved some money. She fell ill and suffered greatly. The next-door neighbour visited her and asked, 'Can I help you?' The old lady asked her to buy a few rice cakes. This surprised the neighbour, seeing the woman had not been able to eat any rice gruel for 10 days. How then could she eat rice cakes? Still wondering, the neighbour went and bought the rice cakes and put them beside the sick woman, and then said goodbye.

Instead of leaving the house, she hid herself, and looked through a hole in the door into the room.

She saw the old woman stir, and take her purse out of her pocket. She then took the gold and silver from her purse, put it into the rice cakes, and swallowed them one by one. 'This is how it will be with anyone who stores up things for himself but is not rich towards God' (Luke 12:21).

Time is fleeting. The life of a man or woman is brief. Many refuse to think about death, saying, 'We cannot take our wives or children with us.' A Japanese priest who always thought of life as a cheap and vain thing nevertheless kept repeating while on his deathbed, 'I don't want to die. I don't want to die.'

In ancient times in Greece there were seven wise men. One of them lost a child and wept inconsolably. Someone tried to comfort him by saying, 'Your tears will not bring your child back.' He answered, 'If weeping could bring my child back I should not be so upset. But my tears won't bring him back, and that is why I am so grieved.'

The Japanese poet Issa, was an honourable man, but when his child died of smallpox he wrote the poem, 'I Know this World is Like the Dew'.

For us, soldiers of Christ, death is not a fearful and sorrowful thing. We are like the son sent from the country to the city to study and be trained there. Our Heavenly Father sent us to the city to be trained, and, just like the son who returns home when his training is completed, so after 50 or 70 years in this world, our souls fly to the Homeland, to our Heavenly Father. For us, that is Heaven.

If the son did not study diligently in the city and spent his days in dissipation, he would fear the return home and the punishment his father would administer. If we rebel against God and live selfish lives, God will judge us and our sin will mean banishment from his presence. Just as the father welcomes home the son who has studied well and attained success, so God will welcome those who have lived according to his will and who have done their part faithfully on earth. He will bestow on them limitless happiness and infinite peace. The Bible says, 'For the wages of sin is death, but the gift of God is eternal life in Christ Jesus our Lord' (Romans 6:23).

For those who have faith in Christ, to die is like passing through a dark stairway to arrive at a bright and wonderful second floor. The apostle Paul declared, 'For to me, to live is Christ and to die is gain' (Philippians 1:21). 'Though outwardly we are wasting away, yet inwardly we are being renewed day by day. For our light and momentary troubles are achieving for us an eternal glory that far outweighs them all. So we fix our eyes not on what is seen, but on what is unseen. For what is seen is temporary, but what is unseen is eternal' (2 Corinthians 4:16-18).

When the apostle Peter was to be crucified he considered himself unworthy to die in the same fashion as Jesus, and asked that he be crucified upside down. In England, a fervent Christian was persecuted by an evil government official who threatened, 'If you don't abandon your faith, you will be put into a bag and thrown into the River Thames.' The Christian replied, 'I'm already on my way to Heaven and I don't mind whether I go by land or sea.'

It is said that Dr Baccus was told he had only half an hour to live, and immediately said, 'Then I will pray for the salvation of the world during the last half hour left to me.' He climbed out of his sick-bed, knelt beside it and died praying.

Mrs General Booth, on her deathbed, declared: 'Now I die under the Salvation Army flag. Comrades, you must live and fight under this flag. God is my salvation and he is my refuge.'

Mr Jo Niijima asked the person at his bedside to read Ephesians 3:20: 'Now to him who is able to do immeasurably more than all we ask or imagine, according to his power that is at work within us.' 'Yes,' he said, 'this is the power. One must trust this power.' That was his last will and testament to his followers and family.

The soldier of God lives in this world. He does his duty to God. He then goes to Heaven after death to receive his crown of glory. How happy is such a life! 'Blessed are the dead who die in the Lord' (Revelation 14:13). So it shall be for all. Let us praise God, our Heavenly Father, and Jesus Christ, our Saviour, and God the Holy Spirit who leads us into all truth.

'For I am already being poured out like a drink offering, and the time has come for my departure. I have fought the good fight, I have finished the race, I have kept the faith. Now there is in store for me the crown of righteousness, which the Lord, the righteous Judge, will award to me on that day – and not only to me, but also to all who have longed for his appearing' (2 Timothy 4:6-8).